A Reading
of
Calvin's *Institutes*

A Reading
of
Calvin's *Institutes*

by
Benjamin A. Reist

Westminster/John Knox Press
Louisville, Kentucky

© 1991 Benjamin A. Reist

Quotations from *Calvin: Institutes of the Christian Religion* (The Library of Christian Classics), edited by John T. McNeill and translated by Ford Lewis Battles, are copyright © MCMLX W. L. Jenkins. Used by permission of Westminster/John Knox Press.

Book design by Ken Taylor

First edition

Published by Westminster/John Knox Press
Louisville, Kentucky

PRINTED IN THE UNITED STATES OF AMERICA
9 8 7 6 5 4 3 2 1

Library of Congress Cataloging-in-Publication Data

Reist, Benjamin A.
   A reading of Calvin's Institutes / by Benjamin A. Reist. — 1st ed.
        p.   cm.
   Includes index.
   ISBN 0-664-25155-2

   1. Calvin, Jean, 1509–1564. Institutio Christianae religionis. 2. Theology, Doctrinal. 3. Reformed Church—Doctrines. I. Title. BX9420.I69R45 1991
230'.42—dc20   90-46623

In memory of my brother
BURTON HORACE REIST
A/C, USAF
(1931–1955)

Contents

INTRODUCTION

The title of this work is deliberate. This is *a* reading of Calvin's *Institutes of the Christian Religion*. It is intended for those who want to make a beginning on the task of becoming participants in the work of systematic theology. Laypersons as well as students who are undertaking the initial phases of their theological education are its intended readers.

This is not to say that specialists with great expertise concerning Calvin's life and thought are not welcome in the following conversation. It is to say that this work is not written with them primarily in mind. This will account for the severe limitation of reference to the vast literature on Calvin in all that follows. I have learned much from that literature. But it is not as a specialist on the Reformation, nor is it as a specialist on the full range of Calvin's writings, that I set out the following line of reflection.

I write as a systematic theologian, one whose work has spanned the second half of the twentieth century. Early in my teaching career at San Francisco Theological Seminary I took over the yearly seminar on Calvin's *Institutes,* and in these latter years, as my work at the seminary approaches its close, I have once again taken up this seminar, now bracketed with the close study of one of the volumes of Karl Barth's

1

Church Dogmatics. In each of these involvements I have found Calvin's comprehensive study of Christian doctrine a remarkably useful means for introducing students to the task of thinking systematically about the doctrines informing their faith. I might note that this is particularly the case when one is moving on to work through Barth's massive lines of theological reflection, but it is by no means restricted to this goal.

So I ask leave of the guild to write with them in the background, not the front seats, of this undertaking. No disrespect is intended, and to those who know their way around this literature it will soon be evident just how deeply indebted I am to the labors of many. It is my hope that students who follow these leads in studying the *Institutes* will find their way into the rich yields of that immense scholarly activity.

I am far less friendly to another set of readers who may look askance at my efforts. In my judgment, Calvin has been done a gross disservice by those practitioners of my own discipline who seek to perpetuate the traditional view of his work. They are the real sources of the bad press this remarkable thinker has received. I state flatly that I regard Calvin as far too important a figure to leave him locked up in this stubborn preserve. I write to show that, properly read, he is a genuine companion in the *contemporary* struggle to make clear the astonishing gospel it is ours to proclaim.

That Calvin is such a companion will come into sharp focus only if we study the *Institutes* with an eye toward discerning his creativity at work. When I was a beginner in the trade, this was possible only for the specialists. The translations available were utterly inaccurate, especially with reference to the fact that Calvin knew the Bible so well that, often quoting it from memory, he equally often misquoted it. These misquotes are invaluable commentaries. Indeed, I truly wish that more of today's preachers were so drenched with the Bible that they could misquote it significantly. Far more important is the fact that until the publication, in 1960, of the McNeill-Battles translation of the *Institutes* only those who commanded Latin could peruse the remarkable accomplishment of Peter Barth and Wilhelm Niesel.

In 1936 Peter Barth and Wilhelm Niesel completed their five-volume edition of selected works of John Calvin. Volumes 3, 4, and 5 of that set contain the text of the 1559 edition of the *Institutes*. This is a critical text, and its most significant feature is that it places before the reader explicit demonstration of the restless creativity always present in Calvin's theological reflections. In all, the *Institutes* went through five principal Latin editions: 1536, 1539, 1543, 1550, and 1559. Each of these editions was accompanied by a French translation from Calvin's own hand. And between these principal editions printings were published that sometimes contained important changes. Calvin was the kind of thinker who never threw away anything. As the editions of the *Institutes* unfolded, he would characteristically pull the text apart and insert new sentences. At crucial points he would shift his expressions. And at even more crucial points he would insert whole new chapters. Most significant of all, he was never at peace on the issue of the doctrine of election. In the final edition he separated it from the doctrine of providence and placed it at the culmination of his discussion of the Christian life.

When two of the most distinguished Calvin scholars of our century, John T. McNeill (as editor) and Ford Lewis Battles (as translator), produced their translation for the Library of Christian Classics (published by Westminster Press as volumes 20 and 21 of this set), they happily took over the decisive feature of the critical apparatus of the Barth-Niesel text of the 1559 edition. This involved backtracking *every* sentence of the final edition, noting the specific edition in which the sentence, or its original form, first appeared. Thus the translation makes it possible to watch the seething ferment of Calvin's thought as one reads. In the process the rigid dogmatician of the bad press disappears. In its place an intellectual companion emerges, risking in his day, as we must in ours, the attempt to formulate Christian doctrine in a way that is both true to its origins and relevant to its context.

Given all of this, the McNeill-Battles translation is today *the only useful English translation.* Add the fact that a comprehensive introduction, elaborate notes, and extensive indexes are part and parcel of this translation. At several points I shall call attention to notes that are particularly significant for this discussion. Obviously, my disclaimer regarding the guild is mitigated with all of this help at hand. This translation is the sole source utilized in this discussion, with the exception of the few instances in which the Latin text is cited (and then it is the Barth-Niesel text that is the source). Throughout the discussion that follows, references to the text will be made in the standard form of notation, with the capital Roman numeral referring to the book, the lowercase Roman numeral referring to the chapter, and the Arabic number referring to the paragraph of a given citation. As a convenience, page numbers to the translation are included in brackets; happily the pagination throughout the two volumes of the translation is continuous. Those who work through this analysis carefully will soon discover why the standard form of reference to the *Institutes* prevails, for by means of it one can immediately place the citation in the unfolding argument that Calvin so meticulously and restlessly developed. Indeed, the best way to use what follows is to have the translation at hand and to read the whole of the *Institutes* while reflecting on this commentary. Note well, also, the policy I have adopted with reference to the present urgency to speak in gender-inclusive language in all that we say. I leave Calvin's text as it stands but write my own reflections in inclusive terms.

The 1559 Latin edition is the definitive edition of the *Institutes*, not because it represented the last word Calvin had to say on the matters at hand, but because he did not live long enough to write another one. This is meant with the utmost seriousness, and it is surely not to be taken facetiously. Calvin's thought was always under way. I shall analyze this final edition in terms of what I call the *parameters* that pervade his reflection in the *Institutes*. These "parameters" are not to be confused with "perimeters," as seems all too often to be the case when the term is misused. The issue is not that of observing *boundaries*; it is, rather, that of discerning the *controlling vectors* that are apparent, in myriad ways, as the discussion unfolds. It is with an eye toward discerning the organismic totality of his thought, and certainly not with the purpose of reducing his system to ideological control, that I utilize this device. I specify fourteen of these parameters. They unfold sequentially, but once discerned, they form a set of vectors, controlling the dynamics of Calvin's thought. The *sequence* of these parameters follows that of the basic outline of the *Institutes*, into four books, which, in a loose way, follows the structure of the Apostles' Creed. But this sequence is not the most important issue at hand. One can get around the whole sweep of the *Institutes* by thinking in terms of the basic themes that are continually interacting as the argument unfolds. Once discerned, these controlling vectors can be understood as operating simultaneously in one of the most comprehensive statements of the understanding of the Christian faith the tradition has given us.

With such a set of intentions I need the apparatus of the McNeill-Battles translation, by which they adapt that of the Barth-Niesel text. At several points, also, the notes that McNeill provides are of pivotal significance, and when they are cited, the page number and the note number give the location in this same translation. The superscripts in the citations indicate the initial source of the passage in question as follows (p. xxvii):

> a: edition of 1536
> b: edition of 1539
> c: edition of 1543
> d: edition of 1550

e: edition of 1559
e(b): edition of 1539 as altered in 1559
e/b: of mixed origin

Citations of the Latin text of the 1559 edition are taken from Petrus Barth and Guilelmus Niesel, eds., *Joannis Calvini Opera Selecta*, Editio secunda emendata (Munich: Chr. Kaiser, 1957, 1959, and 1962), and indicated by the abbreviation *OS*, plus the volume and page numbers.

One final word, and perhaps it is one of the most important: In the discussion that follows, I shall frequently call attention to the Hebraic character of Calvin's argument. This refers to the fact that study of the Old Testament played a decisive role in his understanding of the New Testament, and, accordingly, in his grasp of Christian doctrine. Hebraic thought is intrinsically relational in character, and this is decisive for understanding many of Calvin's most significant insights. We must take care, though, in saying this, to avoid sounding as if we are asserting a view that was quite common in the early days of my own theological studies, namely, the contrasting of Hebraic thought with Hellenic thought, with a clear preference for the former and disdain for the latter. Such a distinction would have been fallacious for Calvin. This reformer was truly a Renaissance man, with a deep grasp of Christian thought as it took shape, under the guidance of scripture, but nevertheless influenced by the Greco-Roman world that was the context within which the thinking of the ancient church developed. If we follow Calvin's argument, we too will be struck by the relational character of the Bible as a whole, and thus we will think in relational

terms. But we will also be faced with the task of seeing
how this relational character, in turn, relates to our
own times and places. We will not be able to do this as
simplistic biblicists for the same reasons that Calvin
himself could not do so in his own time. He accepted
help wherever he could find it, and this help most
certainly included Hellenic ways of thinking. We will
find ourselves engaged with our own contexts with
the same passion as Calvin did if we follow his
example. In so doing, we will be challenged to match
his disciplined creativity with measured risks of our
own. The urgency of doing so is one of the priceless
lessons to be learned from studying the thought of
this remarkable man.

CHAPTER ONE

Reflections on the Knowledge of God, the Significance of Scripture, and the Transcendence of God
—Book I

I. The knowledge of God and the knowledge of humanity are inseparably intertwined.

Celebrated words begin the *Institutes*, and in one form or another they are present throughout each of the editions through which this masterpiece of theological reflection moved:

> b(a)Nearly all the wisdom we possess, that is to say, true and sound wisdom, consists of two parts: the knowledge of God and of ourselves. eBut, while joined by many bonds, bwhich one precedes and brings forth the other is not easy to discern. (I.i.1 [35])

We are dealing with a systematic theologian. Calvin worries about the order in which these interrelated dimensions should be discussed. Indeed, the entirety of the *Institutes* reflects this central concern.

God and humanity must be understood together. This is *the* fundamental assertion in Calvin's theology. Calvin's initial decision is that the knowledge of God has precedence over the knowledge of humanity, since it both generates and conditions it. Even so, the separation between the two is formal, not substantive, for, from our own limited point of view, they will always be intertwined. This leads directly to a decisive delineation in chapter ii of Book I, Calvin's equally celebrated understanding of *piety:*

> e(b/a)Now, the knowledge of God, as I understand it, is that by which we not only conceive that there is a God[e] but also grasp what befits us and is proper to his glory, in fine, what is to our advantage to know of him. Indeed, we shall not say that, properly speaking, God is known where there is no religion or piety. . . . I call "piety" that reverence joined with love of God which the knowledge of his benefits induces. (I.ii.1 [39, 41])

In many ways this is the controlling definition in the *Institutes* as a whole. What Calvin seeks to explore is the *relationship* between God and humanity. "Piety," or "godliness" (as the term is often translated in the text before us; see 39–40 n. 1), characterizes the life of all who would live in this relationship. It is not too much to say that for Calvin the only possible understanding of God and humanity is a *relational* one.

Where does Calvin get this idea? From the Bible. Thus there immediately surfaces the issue so central to all forms of Reformation thought. The word of God as this is heard in Holy Scripture is basic to both the knowledge of God and the knowledge of humanity. Calvin had his own distinctive understanding of this contention. It has left pervasive marks on the Reformed tradition at large. Hence the second parameter:

II. Scripture is necessary for the knowledge of God.

Faithful reflection is the locus of true creativity and devotion. This is intrinsic to Calvin's thought. Such reflection is informed by scripture. The very authority of the scriptures upon which humanity is dependent for its knowledge of God itself depends upon "the secret testimony of the Spirit" (I.vii.4 [78]). This operates in a truly astonishing way. Indeed, the very manner in which it functions may be construed as *the* decisive focus of the fact that the knowledge of God and the knowledge of humanity are intertwined:

> [e]They who strive to build up firm faith in Scripture through disputation are doing things backwards. . . . Even if anyone clears God's Sacred Word from man's evil speaking, he will not at once imprint upon their hearts that certainty which piety requires. . . . The testimony of the Spirit is more excellent than all reason. . . . The same Spirit, therefore, who has spoken through the mouths of the prophets must penetrate into our hearts to persuade us that they faithfully proclaimed what had been divinely commanded. Isaiah very aptly expresses this connection in these words: "My Spirit which is in you, and the words that I have put in your mouth, and the mouths of your offspring, shall never fail" [Isa. 59:21 p.]. (I.vii.4 [79])

To listen to this with modern ears is to hear an overtone in Calvin's formulation that has long escaped notice. We ourselves are profoundly involved in the authenticating of the bases of our conviction. For we, led by the Spirit, establish the connection between the insights of the witness of the past and our own context of faithful reflection.

There is more than meets the eye in this passage. Note well that the text that Calvin cites is from Isaiah. The Old Testament was as significant as the New for Calvin. What is true of him is also true of the Reformed tradition at large. In underscoring this, we encounter the source of that relational understanding of God and humanity so evident in the delineation of true piety. Hebraic thought is intrinsically relational in character. So, therefore, is the thought of the New Testament.

Moreover, in this crucial passage we encounter a fact that is of cardinal significance in dealing with Calvin. He knew the Bible so well that he often quoted it from memory. That is to say, he often misquoted it! Thus it is not too much to say that the scriptural basis of our conviction turns on our own involvement. That this is the way Calvin is quoting Isaiah at this point is indicated by the bracketed reference. Since this issue is so important, we must listen to the translator before moving on:

> A word of explanation needs to be said about the handling of Calvin's Scriptural usage in the present translation. At the outset it became obvious that Calvin more often quotes Scripture *ad sensum* than *ad litteram* and that even when he is quoting directly very often no known Scriptural version is followed verbatim. As a consequence, there has been frequent collation of Scriptural passages with Calvin's Commentaries [Comm.], with the Vulgate [Vg.], the Septuagint [LXX], and the Hebrew.

> Erasmus has also been consulted, and in a few instances (in Proverbs, where no commentary of Calvin exists) parallels with the Geneva Bible have been noted. Even in the same section two different renderings of a verse may be found. When Scripture has been cast in *oratio obliqua*, pronouns shifted, or other slight alteration made by Calvin, the citation has been marked with a "p" and carried in quotation marks. (Page xxiv)

I am really tempted to observe that only those persons who are so drenched with the Bible that they too can significantly misquote it can recognize the depths of the risk involved in relying on the authority of scripture. The relationship between God and the believer is intrinsic to the authority of the word about this relationship.

The word of scripture is intrinsic to the word of God, but it is not identical with it. This is the point at which literalism is always wide of the mark. But the word of scripture is the constant witness to the prior operation of the same faith now demanded of us. Convinced, then, that the same Spirit speaks to us who spoke through the prophets, we take their words as our guide. This is the transcendence of reason for which Calvin contends. Debate cannot establish that connection between reverence and the love of God which "the knowledge of his benefits induces" (I.ii.1)—that is, dispute cannot win the clarification of "that certainty which piety requires" (I.vii.4)—only listening for the word of ultimacy under the guidance of the Spirit of the Ultimate can do this. The third parameter is at hand.

III. The knowledge of God turns on the recognition of the accommodating transcendence of God.

Just as the knowledge of God and the knowledge of humanity are inseparably intertwined, and true piety and the secret testimony of the Holy Spirit on which the authority of scripture depends are themselves intrinsic to each other, so is Calvin's understanding of the transcendence of God implicit in his perception of the relationship between God and us. It is the *present* God who transcends us. Transcendence has to do with the *presence*, not the *remoteness*, of God. All too often we reach for metaphors of remoteness when we try to express God's transcendence of all that God has made. But this denies the very relatedness between God and humanity which is the constant theme of the Bible.

There is a choice demonstration of all of this in Calvin's introduction of the doctrine of the Trinity. Prior to the 1559 edition of the *Institutes* Calvin talked about the Trinity only after he had discussed Christology. For reasons that will stretch our attention later, in the last edition Calvin moved the discussion of Christology to the center of what is now Book II. That the doctrine of the Trinity remains in Book I indicates that unfinished business is at hand, for this doctrine makes sense only in the light of Christology (see 120–121 n.1), and this lends credence to my earlier observation to the effect that the 1559 edition is definitive only because Calvin did not live long enough to write another one.

In spite of the abruptness of the introduction of the Trinity, Calvin's initial points include a truly striking formulation. In rejecting classical errors on the doctrine at hand, Calvin dismissed the so-called Anthropomorphites (an ancient heretical group that claimed that God has human form [see 121 n. 4]) with words that most people would be astonished to find in his writings:

> bFor who even of slight intelligence does not understand that, as nurses commonly do with infants, God is wont in a measure to "lisp" in speaking to us? Thus such forms of speaking do not so much express clearly what God is like as accommodate the knowledge of him to our slight capacity. To do this he must descend far beneath his loftiness. (I.xiii.1 [121])

This says it all. We believe in the lisping God, the ultimate one who will go to any length to relate to us. Here we encounter Calvin's great idea of the *accommodation of God* to us. It will be with us throughout our journey through the *Institutes,* and later we will find it to be the decisive indication of the depths of his Christology, that is, his understanding of the uniqueness and the significance of Jesus confessed to be the Christ. What is to be underscored here is the presence of nearness and remoteness in the same passage. The former entails the accommodation of the latter to our capacity. *This* is the transcendence of God for Calvin.

At this point we come across another of the crucial notes in our translation, an extensive set of observations that includes the following incisive indication:

> The reader will probably look in vain for the noun
> "sovereignty" applied to God in Calvin's writings.
> . . ., although the subject matter usually desig-
> nated thereby appears in the doctrine of Provi-
> dence, which makes frequent use of the traditional
> term "omnipotence" (cf. I.xvi.3). The Beveridge
> and Allen translations of the *Institutes* sometimes
> have introduced the terms "sovereign," "sover-
> eignty," and even inserted the term "decree" in
> accord with orthodox usage, where Calvin's text
> does not contain it. (121 n.1)

More than anything else, this later contention of
Calvinistic orthodoxy lies at the root of the popular
notion of Calvin's thought. Thus the words we have
cited are truly unexpected, and even more, the central
contention they embody is hardly recognized as
Calvin's most basic insight into our limits in the face of
God's transcendence. We know our limits only
because the God who lisps has taught us about them.

At the same time, let it be clearly understood that
this astonishing relationship is not one between
equals. Calvin exhausts his vocabulary in hyperbolic
sweeps in order to emphasize this. Earlier in Book I he
reflects on the fact that humanity itself "is a rare
example of God's power, goodness, and wisdom"
(I.v.3 [54]). This alone should lead us to God. But it
does not, for it produces only a false pride and a
monstrous delusion:

> [e]Do all the treasures of heavenly wisdom concur in
> ruling a five-foot worm while the whole universe
> lacks this privilege? (I.v.4 [56])

We will note other instances of this kind of statement
in Calvin. Be it conceded that his hyperbole is one of

the principal sources of the prevailing stereotyped view of his stern austerity. Did Calvin say that the human being is a "five-foot worm"? Yes. But this is not his final, nor his most important, conclusion on the issue at hand. His basic understanding of humanity is that we are the objects of the accommodation of the God who lisps if need be. He said this too. It is high time that *this* kind of likewise hyperbolic metaphor control all the others.

That God's accommodation to us is the sole source of our knowledge of God is a limit as well as a liberation. For it serves the understanding of God's transcendence of us. Recall again that in the remarkable passage concerning the lisping God, Calvin insists that "such forms of speaking do not so much express clearly what God is like as accommodate the knowledge of him to our slight capacity. To do this he must descend far beneath his loftiness" (I.xiii.1 [121]). As we shall see, for Calvin the heart of the gospel has to do with our certainty that this condescension does in fact take place. Concomitant with this conviction is the faith that whatever else God is, there is no contradiction between God and the accommodation of God to us. This is the only certainty Scripture can give us; it is the only certainty we may claim; to try to go beyond this has deadly implications.

This sense of limit is most important with reference to the doctrine of the Trinity. Calvin's warning is stern:

> bHere, indeed, if anywhere in the secret mysteries of Scripture, we ought to play the philosopher soberly and with great moderation; let us use great caution that neither our thoughts nor our speech

go beyond the limits to which the Word of God
itself extends. For how can the human mind
measure off the measureless essence of God
according to its own little measure, a mind as yet
unable to establish for certain the nature of the
sun's body, though men's eyes daily gaze upon it?
Indeed, how can the mind by its own leading come
to search out God's essence when it cannot even
get to its own? Let us then willingly leave to God
the knowledge of himself. (I.xiii.21 [146])

How do we do this? How do we "leave to God the
knowledge of himself"? We do so by acknowledging
the limit of scripture itself. We remain secure in the
accommodation of God to us and trust the God who
so acts. "We shall be 'leaving it to him' if we conceive
him to be as he reveals himself to us, without
inquiring about him elsewhere than from his Word"
(I.xiii.21 [146]). To attempt to go beyond this is to
enter an endless maze of speculation. Here we
encounter one of Calvin's favorite metaphors, that of
the "labyrinth":

> e(b)But if some distinction does exist in the one
> divinity of Father, Son, and Spirit—something
> hard to grasp—and occasions to certain minds
> more difficulty and trouble than is expedient, elet it
> be remembered that men's minds, when they
> indulge their curiosity, enter into a labyrinth. And
> so let them yield themselves to be ruled by the
> heavenly oracles, even though they may fail to
> capture the height of the mystery. (I.xiii.21 [146–
> 147])

This brings to mind a marvelous aside later on:
"When a certain shameless fellow mockingly asked a

pious old man what God had done before the creation of the world, the latter aptly countered that he had been building hell for the curious" (I.xiv.1 [160]).

We have contended that for Calvin the transcendence of humanity has to do with the presence, not the remoteness, of God. Nowhere is this more emphatically the case than in his understanding of the necessary interrelationship between creation and providence:

> [b]Even though the minds of the impious too are compelled by merely looking upon earth and heaven to rise up to the Creator, yet faith has its own peculiar way of assigning the whole credit for Creation to God. . . . For unless we pass on to his providence—however we may seem both to comprehend with the mind and to confess with the tongue—we do not yet properly grasp what it means to say: "God is Creator." (I.xvi.1 [197])

Here we must move very carefully, and here once again there is a vast difference between reading Calvin and reading about him. To be sure, he does indeed believe in the omnipotence of God. But what kind of omnipotence? It is one "engaged in ceaseless activity" (I.xvi.3 [200]). Note well the present tense in which this statement is uttered. And note well the same dimension in what immediately follows:

> [e]Not, indeed, an omnipotence that is only a general principle of confused motion, as if he were to command a river to flow through its once-appointed channels, but one that is directed toward individual and particular motions. [b]For he is deemed omnipotent, not because he can indeed act, yet sometimes ceases and sits in idleness, [e(b)]or

> continues by a general impulse that order of nature
> which he previously appointed; but because,
> governing heaven and earth by his providence, he
> so regulates all things that nothing takes place
> without his deliberation. (I.xvi.3 [200])

Such an understanding is a function of faith, and
not only that, but faith *in Christ*, in whom we will later
hear Calvin say the decisive accommodation of God to
us occurs. Since it is a function of faith, it can have
nothing to do with fortune or chance; that is, it cannot
be self-evident:

> eCarnal reason ascribes all such happenings,
> whether prosperous or adverse, to fortune. But
> anyone who has been taught by Christ's lips that
> all the hairs of his head are numbered [Matt. 10:30]
> will look farther afield for a cause and will consider
> that all events are governed by God's secret plan.
> (I.xvi.2 [199])

✓The primary reason this is so is that providence is
not a general principle. It is an implication of the faith
the scriptures proclaim and demand. The *present* God
rules. The issue is not prior knowledge but active
presence. As Calvin insists in a memorable line, and
how one wishes that this were remembered by all
who refer to him, pro or con:

> eProvidence is lodged in the act; e(b)for many babble
> too ignorantly of bare foreknowledge. (I.xvi.4
> [202])

✓Metaphors of spatial distance and mysterious
remoteness found their way into the inner realms of
Calvinistic orthodoxy, where they remain indelibly
fixed. However, this is not true to Calvin's most

pivotal insights. And this is why Calvin is too important a figure to be left to the Calvinists. We cannot sustain this claim, though, with only Book I before us, for to discern the depths of these issues we must turn to his Christology. This is the fulcrum of Book II, indeed of the *Institutes* as a whole.

CHAPTER TWO

Reflections on the Sinfulness of Humanity, Christ the Mediator, the Three Uses of the Law, and the Threefold Office of Christ
—Book II

IV. We have lost a freedom only the Spirit can restore.

Book II of the *Institutes* is entitled "The Knowledge of God the Redeemer in Christ, First Disclosed to the Fathers Under the Law and Then to Us in the Gospel." Christology, however, is not the sole subject of Book II. The initial issue discussed is the doctrine of the sinfulness of humanity. To be sure, the question of the sinfulness of humanity is intrinsic to any treatment of the uniqueness and the significance of confessing Jesus of Nazareth to be the Christ. But in taking up the question of sin *before* dealing with Christology itself, Calvin encountered real problems, as will anyone who follows this procedure, for faith in Christ is the presupposition for understanding the sinfulness of sin. Two later figures who were influenced heavily by Calvin's thought, Friedrich Schleier-

macher and Karl Barth, would address this problem
directly, but that is another story.

Calvin stood squarely within the Augustinian
tradition when it came to understanding both the
human predicament and its resolution, for he was
absolutely convinced that humanity is totally dependent upon God for the restoration of what has been
lost. For Calvin, this meant wrestling, on his own,
with the problem of the freedom of the will, and his
conclusion was that whereas we are free to will
whatever we may wish, we are not free to achieve that
which we need most of all, the restoration of the
freedom to live before God as those knowing the
salvation that is God's greatest gift.

Thus Calvin took over Augustine's insight that we
are "indeed free but not freed" (II.ii.8 [266]). At this
point it will be worth our while to backtrack for a
moment to a pivotal set of remarks in Book I.
Wrestling with the attempt to understand the nature
of humanity, Calvin followed Augustine on the
vexatious question of free will. All was well in
humanity's beginnings:

> eMan in his first condition excelled in these
> pre-eminent endowments, so that his reason,
> understanding, prudence, and judgment not only
> sufficed for the direction of his earthly life, but by
> them men mounted up even to God and eternal
> bliss. (I.xv.8 [195])

But then "choice" was added, in order to "make the
will completely amenable to the guidance of reason."
The basic Augustinian maneuver then sets in in
Calvin's thought:

> eIn this integrity man by free will had the power, if
> he so willed, to attain eternal life. Here it would be
> out of place to raise the question of God's secret
> predestination because our present subject is not
> what can happen or not, but what man's nature
> was like. Therefore Adam could have stood if he
> wished, seeing that he fell solely by his own will.
> (I.xv.8 [195])

Note carefully that Calvin refuses to treat what could
have happened. He is preoccupied with the nature of
the case *now*. The human predicament now observa-
ble is the result of the free exercise of the human will.
And this situation is made all the more intense by our
attempt to reckon with it short of the gospel:

> eHence the great obscurity faced by the philoso-
> phers, for they were seeking in a ruin for a
> building, and in scattered fragments for a well-knit
> structure. They held this principle, that man would
> not be a rational animal unless he possessed free
> choice of good and evil; also it entered their minds
> that the distinction between virtues and vices
> would be obliterated if man did not order his life by
> his own planning. Well reasoned so far—if there
> had been no change in man. But since this was
> hidden from them, it is no wonder they mix up
> heaven and earth! (I.xv.8 [195–196])

The trouble is that there has been a change in
humanity. And this change is both pervasive and
permanent. In Augustine's phrase, "the will is indeed
free but not freed: free of righteousness but enslaved
to sin!" (II.ii.8 [266]). How so? The heart of Calvin's
long discussion of these issues is to be found in the
last six paragraphs of the opening chapter of Book II.
That the discussion of Adam is actually the discussion

of human nature at large is the obvious assertion in the following lines:

> bWe must surely hold that Adam was not only the progenitor but, as it were, the root of human nature; and that therefore in his corruption mankind deserved to be vitiated. (II.i.6 [248])

The decisive point immediately follows, for Calvin draws directly on Romans 5:12 to insist that Adam and Christ must be understood together, in such a way that the second Adam is the clue to the significance of the first. Calvin uses the foil of the Pelagian error to make this clear:

> bWhat nonsense will the Pelagians chatter here? That Adam's sin was propagated by imitation? Then does Christ's righteousness benefit us only as an example set before us to imitate? Who can bear such sacrilege! But if it is beyond controversy that Christ's righteousness, and thereby life, are ours by communication, it immediately follows that both were lost in Adam, only to be recovered in Christ; and that sin and death crept in through Adam, only to be abolished through Christ. (II.i.6 [248])

In the strength of the knowledge of redemption, Calvin can face, and so can we, the full ravages of the human contradiction that is sin. What is not natural enters the natural arena and becomes so pervasive and permanent that it seems to be natural in and of itself. Thus Calvin can state his own paradox:

> bTherefore we declare that man is corrupted through natural vitiation, but a vitiation that did not flow from nature. (II.i.11 [254])

A severe technical difficulty is involved in handling this passage, so much so that here we have need for another of those decisive notes from our translation. This has to do with the ambiguity of Calvin's use of the term "natural." When this first occurs, in I.ii.2 [37], the editor observes:

> Calvin uses the words "nature," "natural," and "by nature" in two very different senses: (1) "Nature" may mean created perfection in which there is no evil . . . ; or (2) "nature" may mean the state of man and angels after having fallen from perfection . . . and clearly distinguished from the former in II.i.10, 11. The opening sentence of II.i.11 places the two uses side by side. This distinction is indispensable for understanding the relation of God to creation and to sin. (38 n. 7)

We must remember throughout our reflections on this passage that *both* of these meanings of "nature" stand side by side in these opening lines of II.i.11. Overlooking this ambiguity inexorably leads to the misunderstanding of Calvin's view of the limits of humanity. These limits are severe indeed, but they are not the result of divine creativity that is either malicious or sadistic. They are the result of the operation of the will of humanity itself. This insight is directly rooted in the gospel itself. For Calvin as for Paul, the second Adam is the clue to the first. With this contention—that what is not natural enters the natural arena in such a permanent and pervasive way that it seems natural—Calvin was delivered, as was Augustine, from dualism as the solution to the problem of sin. Calvin replicates Augustine in rejecting the Manichean error:

> ᵇThus vanishes the foolish trifling of the Man-
> ichees, who, when they imagined wickedness of
> substance in man, dared fashion another creator
> for him in order that they might not seem to assign
> the cause and beginning of evil to the righteous
> God. (II.i.11 [254–255])

No dualism is necessary. There is no independent
principle of evil in the gospel. The doctrine of sin is
profoundly retrospective in character, for it is in the
light of the Christ that what occurred in Adam
becomes clear.

Unfinished business is still at hand, though, in our
citing of the "free but not freed" passage above. Calvin
had a genuine sense of *discomfort* with this paradoxical
formulation. The fact is that his grasp of human
limitations was accompanied by a high estimate of the
human capacities. This turns on distinguishing between human understanding and the exercising of the
human will. Here we encounter his own version of
Augustine's paradoxical insight. *Humility* must be the
abiding mark of our consciousness of all that we have
and are:

> ᵇA saying of Chrysostom's has always pleased me
> very much, that the foundation of our philosophy
> is humility. But that of Augustine pleases me even
> more: "When a certain rhetorician was asked what
> was the chief rule in eloquence, he replied,
> 'Delivery'; what was the second rule, 'Delivery';
> what was the third rule, 'Delivery'; so if you ask me
> concerning the precepts of the Christian religion,
> first, second, third, and always I would answer,
> 'Humility.' " (II.ii.11 [268–269])

And yet, at the same time, fallen though we may be, the human mind bears the marks of the gift of God, for, as regards art and science,

> bwhenever we come upon these matters in secular writers, let that admirable light of truth shining in them teach us that the mind of man, though fallen and perverted from its wholeness, is nevertheless clothed and ornamented with God's excellent gifts. If we regard the Spirit of God as the sole fountain of truth, we shall neither reject the truth itself, nor despise it wherever it shall appear, unless we wish to dishonor the Spirit of God. (II.ii.15 [273–274])

It is fascinating to contemplate the sense in which *all* truth, by whomever discerned, is rooted in the Spirit of God. Faith can hardly debate this. But the source of faith itself is beyond the direct grasp of human understanding. This is its decisive limit, as Calvin carefully indicated and relentlessly elaborated:

> bWe must now analyze what human reason can discern with regard to God's Kingdom and to spiritual insight. This spiritual insight consists chiefly in three things: (1) knowing God; (2) knowing his fatherly favor in our behalf, in which our salvation consists; (3) knowing how to frame our life according to the rule of his law. In the first two points—and especially in the second—the greatest geniuses are blinder than moles! (II.ii.18 [277])

Can the point at hand be overstated? No! But it can be taken out of context. It is with reference to the spiritual insight, the deep conviction that God is love, that "the greatest geniuses are blinder than moles." Once again note Calvin's hyperbole. But do not miss his insight. Strictly in the light of the gospel, and by its strength alone, Calvin can conclude that

> bhuman reason . . . neither approaches, nor strives toward, nor even takes a straight aim at, this truth: to understand who the true God is or what sort of God he wishes to be toward us. (II.ii.18 [278])

Hence, then, our need for the guidance of the Spirit:

> eTo sum up, much as man desires to follow what is good, still he does not follow it. There is no man to whom eternal blessedness is not pleasing, yet no man aspires to it except by the impulsion of the Holy Spirit. (II.ii.26 [286–287])

How does this guidance of the Spirit take shape? With Calvin's insistence on the secret testimony of the Spirit as the base of the authority of scripture, the first half of the answer to this question is already clear. It gains concrete form with the proclamation of the gospel which is the heart of the content of the scriptural witness. The second half of the answer to this question entails, then, the statement of the christological fulcrum, upon which the whole of Calvin's theology depends. For it is only in Christ that we can know God as our Father. This brings us to the decisive center, not only of Book II but of the whole of the *Institutes*.

V. Faith in Christ is decisive for our redeeming knowledge of God.

Calvin's restless theological creativity was always under way. Each of the editions of the *Institutes* commences with an address to the readers. For each new edition he notes that new material has been included, and then adds:

> e(b)Although I did not regret the labor spent, I was never satisfied until the work had been arranged in the order now set forth. (Page 3)

I am convinced that as of 1559 one of the decisive reasons behind this remark is before us in chapter vi of Book II, appearing for the first time in the 1559 edition. There can be little doubt that Christology is the center, the fulcrum, of Calvin's thought as a whole. Here, at the apex of his theological productivity, we have *the* choice expression of this fact. The opening lines of this new chapter make the unequivocal claim that all that has been said in the *Institutes* so far depends upon what must be said now:

> eThe whole human race perished in the person of Adam. Consequently that original excellence and nobility which we have recounted would be of no profit to us but would rather redound to our greater shame, until God, who does not recognize as his handiwork men defiled and corrupted by sin, appeared as Redeemer in the person of his only-begotten Son. Therefore, since we have fallen from life unto death, the whole knowledge of God the Creator that we have discussed would be useless unless faith also followed, setting forth for us God our Father in Christ. (II.vi.1 [340–341])

We are at the nerve center of the *Institutes*. Though ostensibly following the outline of the Apostles' Creed, albeit in a loose fashion, the fact is that the argument of the *Institutes* as a whole has two parts. This is the turning point into the second, and more

extensive, section of Calvin's comprehensive discussion of Christian doctrine. This is why this single,
brief chapter merits a "parameter" unto itself alone.

In this chapter Calvin sets out two decisive
specifications concerning the centrality of Christology
for all Christian reflection. The first of these has to do
with the impasse of attempting to discern the depths
of our knowledge of God apart from the fact of Christ:

> eEven if God wills to manifest his fatherly favor to
> us in many ways, yet we cannot by contemplating
> the universe infer that he is Father. Rather,
> conscience presses us within and shows in our sin
> just cause for his disowning us and not regarding
> or recognizing us as his sons. (II.vi.1 [341])

This is an astonishing claim. Contemplation of the
universe, however moving, cannot deliver us from the
voice of doom pervading our consciences. The sinful
predicament of humanity cannot be overcome by awe
alone. This is why it is the case that "after the fall of the
first man no knowledge of God apart from the Mediator
has had power unto salvation" (II.vi.1 [341]).

Hence the second specification: Faith in Christ
equals faith in God. This one-to-one equation is the
very heart of Calvin's Christology. Calvin's claim is
that Jesus the Christ is *the one and only mediator* by
whom God is known as Father. This is why it can and
must be said that faith in Christ and faith in God are
one and the same thing:

> eChrist himself bade his disciples believe in him,
> that they might clearly and perfectly believe in
> God: "You believe in God; believe also in me"
> [John 14:1]. For even if, properly speaking, faith

mounts up from Christ to the Father, yet he means this: although faith rests in God, it will gradually disappear unless he who retains it in perfect firmness intercedes as Mediator. Otherwise, God's majesty is too lofty to be attained by mortal men, who are like grubs crawling upon the earth. (II.vi.4 [346])

By now the hyperbole need not deter us. But do note that what Calvin is thinking of is the *limit of the human capacity, not just its sinfulness*. This is one of the truly decisive points to emerge at the apex of Calvin's thought. Human limitation and human sinfulness are intertwined, but they are not identical. At this crucial point, he speaks primarily of *limited* humanity in thinking of the mediator's indispensable role in our redemption.

This is why Calvin insists that "apart from Christ the saving knowledge of God does not stand" (II.vi.4 [347]). And it is also why this fourth paragraph of the chapter contains as its own central pivot the very idea of God's accommodation to us that we have already seen to be one of his most significant insights into the knowledge of God:

eIn this sense Irenaeus writes that the Father, himself infinite, becomes finite in the Son, for he has accommodated himself to our little measure lest our minds be overwhelmed by the immensity of his glory. Fanatics, not reflecting upon this, twist a useful statement into an impious fantasy, as if there were in Christ only a portion of divinity, outflowing from the whole perfection of God. Actually, it means nothing else than that God is comprehended in Christ alone. John's saying has always been true: "He that does not have the Son does not have the

> Father" [I John 2:23 p.]. For even if many men once
> boasted that they worshiped the Supreme Majesty,
> the Maker of heaven and earth, yet because they
> had no Mediator it was not possible for them truly to
> taste God's mercy, and thus be persuaded that he
> was their Father. (II.vi.4 [347])

It is impossible to specify more significant lines than these in Calvin's thought. The Christ is the indispensable link between God and humanity. The Mediator is a function of our limitations. Without the Christ we cannot *comprehend* God. The issue is relationship, not substance. This is why it is pointless to ask how much of God do we have in Christ. What we have is a contact. This is how Calvin reads 1 John 2:23 in another of those marvelous misquotations of scripture in the *Institutes*.

Taken together, these two specifications indicate the relational character of Calvin's Christology. In saying this, we lay hold of the basically Hebraic nature of this thought as a whole. In the Old Testament, and therefore in the New, the primary subject is the relationship between God and humanity. Christ is the center of this for Calvin. But given the Hebraic character of his conviction, it can come as no surprise that he proceeds now to the discussion of the law in the light of the gospel.

VI. The law must be understood in the light of Christ; hence the principal use of the law is that of instruction and exhortation.

The decisive point is in front of us immediately, for it has to do with the *necessary* sequence of the argument. Calvin insists that we think of *gospel and law*, not *law and gospel* as Luther would have it. This is one of the basic differentiations between the Lutheran and the Reformed traditions, and its historic significance cannot be overemphasized. More of that later; the crucial issue here is that this line of argument is the reason behind the insertion of the sixth chapter of Book II in the 1559 edition of the *Institutes*. Thus the initial implication of insisting, as has been done with the fifth parameter of the argument, that Christology is the fulcrum of Calvin's thought is primarily *ethical* in character.

In saying this, we must always bear in mind that the term "law" in Calvin's thought has a variety of meanings. It does not refer just to the Decalogue; it may mean, as well, the entirety of life under the Torah, as this pervades the central concerns of the Old Testament, and it may also entail the legal tradition of the medieval world as Calvin knew it (see 354 n. 9). It is fascinating to reflect on the fact that the difference between Lutheranism and the Reformed tradition at this point has to do with the lives of the two Reformers in question: Luther's background was that of an Augustinian monk, Calvin's initial training had to do with the study of the law.

This far too simple biographical reference is hardly sufficient to disclose the real depths of the matter at hand, but it does facilitate the exposition of the issues involved. Calvin, functioning as a second-generation reformer, and in the context of Geneva's search for self-understanding as a city-state with a century-old history of breaking with its past, moved in a direction that would have massive significance for subsequent developments in the history of the West, and even beyond it. In all of this he was *building* on the pioneering work of Luther, without which none of this would ever have surfaced in the way it did.

The gospel/law progression in Calvin's thought led him to an extremely significant addition to the line of reflection he took over from Luther. Luther had spoken of *two* uses of the law; Calvin added a third, which he explicitly regarded as the most important. The *first* use has to do with convicting humanity of its failure to please God:

> b(a)Let us survey briefly the function and use of what is called the "moral law." Now, so far as I understand it, it consists of three parts.
>
> The first part is this: while it shows God's righteousness, that is, the righteousness alone acceptable to God, it warns, informs, convicts, and lastly condemns, every man of his own unrighteousness. (II.vii.6 [354])

This first "use" directly implies the second: *condemnation* evokes *restraint:*

> bThe second function of the law is this: aat least by fear of punishment to restrain certain men who are untouched by any care for what is just and right unless compelled by hearing the dire threats in the law. (II.vii.10 [358])

If, as was the case with Luther, these two uses alone prevail, then law and gospel will stand in a perfect, dialectical tension. So to understand them opens the way to Luther's incisive breakthrough, the discerning of the inexhaustible significance of Paul's understanding of *justification by grace through faith alone*. But for Calvin the question becomes, How does one *live out* this justification? and the beginning of his answer to this complex question generated his celebrated "third use" of law, the one that he regarded as involving the decisive meaning of the law for our lives. It has to do with nothing less than the presence of the Spirit (over and over we recognize this basic motif in Calvin's thought):

> [b]The third and principal use, which pertains more closely to the proper purpose of the law, [b(a)]finds its place among believers in whose hearts the Spirit of God already lives and reigns. (II.vii.12 [360])

Believers—that is, those in whom the Spirit of God "already lives"—"profit by the law in two ways." In stating, and then elaborating, these two factors, Calvin transmutes the law from a negative to a positive significance. First:

> [b(a)]Here is the best instrument for them to learn more thoroughly each day the nature of the Lord's will to which they aspire, and to confirm them in the understanding of it. [a]It is as if some servant, already prepared with all earnestness of heart to commend himself to his master, [b(a)]must search out and observe his master's ways more carefully in order to conform and accommodate himself to them. (II.vii.12 [360])

This positive significance of the law does not diminish the forcefulness of the first two uses. Calvin's reputation for austerity is well earned: "The law is to the flesh like a whip to an idle and balky ass, to arouse it to work" (II.vii.12 [361]). Even so, the second factor in the third use has a positive function; it is that of exhorting the faithful to the very possibility

of following the guidance that the first factor envisions:

> [b]Again, because we need not only teaching but also
> exhortation, the servant of God will also avail
> himself of this benefit of the law: by frequent
> meditation upon it to be aroused to obedience, be
> strengthened in it, and be drawn back from the
> slippery path of transgression. (II.vii.12 [360–361])

The three uses of the law are present in Calvin's
thought from the beginning. But with the 1559 edition
of the *Institutes* a telling clarification set in—they are
introduced *before* the exposition of the Ten Commandments rather than following it, as had been the case in
prior editions. This clarifies a line of reflection that is
far more important than it may appear at first. Calvin
numbered the commandments differently from Luther and the Catholic tradition before him (see 378 n.
16). This structured the tradition of studying the "two
tables" of the law, and this was precisely the problem
for Calvin:

> [b]We ought to ponder what the division of the
> divine law into two Tables meant. . . . In the First
> Table, God instructs us in piety and the proper
> duties of religion, by which we are to worship his
> majesty. The Second Table prescribes how in
> accordance with the fear of his name we ought to
> conduct ourselves in human society. [a]In this way
> our Lord, as the Evangelists relate, summarizes the
> whole law under two heads: that "we should love
> the Lord our God with all our heart, and with all
> our soul, and with all our powers"; and "that we
> should love our neighbor as ourselves" [Luke 10:27
> p.; Matt. 22:37, 39]. [b]You see that of the two parts

> in which the law consists, one he directs to God;
> the other he applies to men. (II.viii.11 [376–377])

This doubly valenced demand of the law caused Calvin no problem, but the neat numbering of the Decalogue did. The Bible is clear only on the number, but not the numbering. And the tradition's solution to this problem left out something decisive for him:

> ᵇThat the law is divided into ten words is beyond doubt, for on the authority of God himself this has often been confirmed. Thus we are uncertain, not about the number, but about the way of dividing the Decalogue. ᵇ⁽ᵃ⁾Those who so divide them as to give three precepts to the First Table and relegate the remaining seven to the Second, erase from the number the commandment concerning images, or at least hide it under the First. There is no doubt that the Lord gave it a distinct place as a commandment, ᵃyet they absurdly tear in two the Tenth Commandment about not coveting the possessions of one's neighbor. (II.viii.12 [378])

Thus Calvin factored off the commandment concerning "no graven images" into a separate entity having weight equal to the other nine words. Why was this so important for him?

> ᵇThe purpose of this [Second] commandment, then, is that he does not will that his lawful worship be profaned by superstitious rites. To sum up, he wholly calls us back and withdraws us from petty carnal observances, which our stupid minds, crassly conceiving of God, are wont to devise. And then he makes us conform to his lawful worship, that is, a spiritual worship established by himself. Moreover, he marks the grossest fault in this transgression, outward idolatry. (II.viii.17 [383])

Mundane matters invade the spiritual realm for Calvin. The proper worship of God has no room for "petty carnal observances," the identification of which is entirely a *this-worldly affair*. Idolatry takes place here, where we are, in this world. Conflict with it is a matter of the first magnitude, so much so that it is part and parcel of the *first* table of the law. That this concern left an indelible mark on the Reformed tradition as far as liturgy is concerned is obvious. What is not so obvious is that it is consonant with Calvin's addition of a third use to the two uses of the law he took over from Luther. As has already been indicated, Calvin replaced the dialectical tension between law and gospel with the progression from gospel to law. So it is that the discussion of the law in its three uses paves the way for a return to the further analysis of Christology, with which Book II concludes.

VII. The gospel/law relationship evokes a clear and profound Christology.

Calvin remained true to the tradition clarified at Nicaea and Chalcedon in working out the Christology that informed his understanding of the relationship between gospel and law. Our human predicament is such that only in terms of the Mediator, who is "both true God and true man," can we know that God is indeed with us. Faith alone can discern the reason why this is so, for it is rooted not in some abstract necessity but in the love of God alone:

> [b(a)]Now it has been of the greatest importance for us that he who was to be our Mediator is both true

God and true man. [e]If someone asks why this is necessary, there has been no simple (to use the common expression) or absolute necessity. Rather, it has stemmed from a heavenly decree, on which men's salvation depended. Our most merciful Father decreed what was best for us. (II.xii.1 [464])

Calvin's way of stating the astonishing content of God's decision to be for us contains a memorable formulation:

[a]The situation would surely have been hopeless had the very majesty of God not descended to us, since it was not in our power to ascend to him. Hence, it was necessary for the Son of God to become for us "Immanuel, that is, God with us" [Isa. 7:14; Matt. 1:23], [e(b/a)]and in such a way that his divinity and our human nature might by mutual connection grow together. [b(a)]Otherwise the nearness would not have been near enough, nor the affinity sufficiently firm, for us to hope that God might dwell with us. (II.xii.1 [464–465])

Here very close scrutiny of the text demands our attention. Calvin ponders at length the meaning of Isaiah's phrase, "Immanuel, that is, God with us." God must come to us if we are to be with God. So it is that the very heart of the gospel is that God is indeed with us. But how does this happen? The lines immediately following the citation represent a new crystallization of Calvin's contention that the Christ is the mediator between God and us. For these words are new in 1559. From the editions of 1536 and 1539 on, Calvin had said that Isaiah's text means "that just as his divinity joins us *(adiungebat)* so our humanity unites with *(copularet)* his divinity." Now he says the passage indicates that God is with us "in such a way

that his divinity and our humanity might by mutual
connection grow together *[ut mutua coniunctione eius
divinitas et hominum natura inter se coalescerent]*" (*OS*
3:437). This new language reflects the clarification
regarding Christology that sets in with chapter vi of
Book II, also new in 1559, as we have seen. Having
rewritten this crucial phrase, Calvin proceeded with
the claim he had made from 1536 forward: "Otherwise the nearness would not have been near enough,
nor the affinity sufficiently firm, for us to hope that
God might dwell with us." Then he continues:

> [e(a)]So great was the disagreement between our
> uncleanness and God's perfect purity! [e]Even if man
> had remained free from all stain, his condition
> would have been too lowly for him to reach God
> without a Mediator. (II.xii.1 [465])

The significance of this unfolding clarification is
crucial. Note that Calvin has now refined his understanding of the depths of the gospel. The accommodation of God to us, which we saw to be so pivotal for
II.vi.4, correlates not just with the sinfulness of humanity but with its *limits*. "Immanuel, that is, God
with us" had been grasped, but *only in terms of
the difference between God and us*. Hence the 1536/1539
phraseology of Calvin's interpretation used different
verbs for God, on the one hand, and for us, on the
other. In 1559 Calvin understands the "nearness that
is near enough" and the "affinity" that is "sufficiently
firm" for us truly to hope that God is "with us" in
much more emphatic terms. God is with us in such a
way that God and we "by mutual connection grow

together." The same phrase applies both to God and to us.

Dare we say that for Calvin it was becoming clear that as God grows, so do we? If so, dare we say that in the light of Calvin's insights we may now risk the view that our own growth is the result of, even a clue to, God's growth? We may, but only with tools now available to us. Here we encounter the *processive* character of Calvin's Christology. And our thinking must be rigorously disciplined in making this observation. Calvin's thought is processive because it is relational. And it is relational because it is profoundly Hebraic. *Isaiah's* text informs his Christology. The sinfulness of humanity is in the picture. But the decisive hues of Calvin's Christology have to do with the God who relates to us *in terms of our limited human capacities.* To read II.vi.4 and II.xii.1 in close juxtaposition is to discern one of the most far-reaching implications of the argument of the *Institutes* in its final form.

In the light of all of this, the depths of Calvin's long celebrated contribution to our understanding of the uniqueness and significance of Jesus confessed to be the Christ comes into view. This is his discussion of Christ's threefold office:

> eIn order that faith may find a firm basis for salvation in Christ, and thus rest in him, this principle must be laid down: the office enjoined upon Christ by the Father consists of three parts. For he was given to be prophet, king, and priest. (II.xv.1. [494])

The *prophetic* office turns on the fact that Jesus the Christ, just as the prophets before him, was anointed the task of teaching, thus bearing witness to the grace of God. Here the crucial passage contains a decisive note that must not be overlooked, for it anticipates the central component of Calvin's doctrine of the church. Moreover, the *finality* of the Christ's prophetic office, putting an end to prophecy, is a deliverance into the continuum of the proclamation of the gospel of this same Christ. What, then, is brought to an end is not the inexhaustible depths of the response of the faithful to what God does in Christ but rather their need of anything more than what is being accomplished in him through the Spirit:

> eWe see that he was anointed by the Spirit to be herald and witness of the Father's grace. And that not in the common way—for he is distinguished from other teachers with a similar office. On the other hand, we must note this: he received anointing, not only for himself that he might carry out the office of teaching, but for his whole body that the power of the Spirit might be present in the continuing preaching of the gospel. This, however, remains certain: the perfect doctrine he has brought has made an end to all prophecies. . . . That is, outside Christ there is nothing worth knowing, and all who by faith perceive what he is like have grasped the whole immensity of heavenly benefits. (II.xv.2 [496])

This "continuing preaching of the gospel" which *we* are to undertake indicates the processive character of the first office of the Christ. For the task of the first office is not completed by him.

The *kingly* office must be understood to be "spiritual in nature," having to do with the power of

Christ, through which the "whole force and eternity" of his work is given to us:

> eI come now to kingship. It would be pointless to speak of this without first warning my readers that it is spiritual in nature. For from this we infer its efficacy and benefit for us, as well as its whole force and eternity. . . . But this eternity is also of two sorts or must be considered in two ways: the first pertains to the whole body of the church; the second belongs to each individual member. (II.xv.3 [496–497])

For the second time, the relationship to the doctrine of the church is explicit and primary, and its elaboration is decisive for Calvin's understanding of both the work of Christ and its significance for the faithful. Thus two steps are taken. First:

> eGod surely promises here that through the hand of his Son he will be the eternal protector and defender of his church. . . . Therefore, whenever we hear of Christ as armed with eternal power, let us remember that the perpetuity of the church is secure in this protection. (II.xv.3 [497])

Second, in this light our ultimate hope is secured:

> eNow with regard to the special application of this to each one of us—the same "eternity" ought to inspire us to hope for blessed immortality. (II.xv.3 [498])

But precisely because we are speaking of the kingship of Christ, which is truly spiritual, this hope is *conditioned*, since it entails life under the sign of the cross, the drastic ambiguities of which can know only an ultimacy that transcends the present:

eWe have said that we can perceive the force and usefulness of Christ's kingship only when we recognize it to be spiritual. This is clear enough from the fact that, while we must fight throughout life under the cross, our condition is harsh and wretched. What, then, would it profit us to be gathered under the reign of the Heavenly King, unless beyond this earthly life we were certain of enjoying its benefits? (II.xv.4 [498])

Hence the need for explicating the *priestly* office of Christ and thus to clarify, as explicitly as possible, the necessity of speaking of Christ as mediator. The predicament of humanity is such that apart from this the work of Christ as both prophet and king would not be ours. This carries further into the depths of faithful insight what we have already heard Calvin claim: Awe, even admiration, cannot in themselves persuade us that God is the merciful One who effects our reconciliation:

eNow we must speak briefly concerning the purpose and use of Christ's priestly office: as a pure and stainless Mediator he is by his holiness to reconcile us to God. But God's righteous curse bars our access to him, and God in his capacity as judge is angry toward us. Hence, an expiation must intervene in order that Christ as priest may obtain God's favor for us and appease his wrath. Thus Christ to perform this office had to come forward with a sacrifice. (II.xv.6 [501])

We dare not stop with the passage before us, lest its negative hues color once and for all Calvin's understanding of the priestly office of Christ. These negative hues derive from scripture, but there too the final outcome receives the intensely positive impact of ultimate redemption. Moreover, Calvin knows well the tradition he serves, and thus Anselm's work is in the background of his labors. Even so, this "principal point on which . . . our whole salvation turns" is rooted in the graceful will of God, and whereas "we must begin from the death of Christ in order that the efficacy and benefit of his priesthood may reach us," the blessing that is ours is the foretaste of the promise of the kingly office itself.

> [e]It follows that he is an everlasting intercessor: through his pleading we obtain favor. Hence arises not only trust in prayer, but also peace for godly consciences, while they safely lean upon God's fatherly mercy and are surely persuaded that whatever has been consecrated through the Mediator is pleasing to God. (II.xv.6 [502])

And here also, just as with the first two aspects of the threefold office of Christ, the explicit connection of all of this to the doctrine of the church is given forceful affirmation:

> [e(b/a)]Now, Christ plays the priestly role, not only to render the Father favorable and propitious toward us by an eternal law of reconciliation, but also to receive us as his companions in this great office [Rev. 1:6]. For we who are defiled in ourselves, yet are priests in him . . . (II.xv.6 [502])

In a manner, then, that resonates in the depths with the same kind of reflection that led Calvin beyond the negative impact of the first two uses of the law to the inexhaustibly positive meaning of its third use, Calvin's understanding of Christology takes its final shape. His insight into the work of Christ, though admitting no relaxation of reckoning with the drastic condition of humanity apart from the love of God, yields a profoundly positive grasp of the possibility of life in the mode of ultimacy. This, as will become clear, is the most accurate way to deal with the central concern of Book III.

CHAPTER THREE

Reflections on Life
in the Presence of the Spirit
—Book III

VIII. Faith must be defined in terms of Christ, the Spirit, and the believer's radical commitment.

How do we take part in all that about which we have spoken so far? Or, to use more classical language, how is it that we receive the benefits of Christ, of which we have heard in the proclamation of the gospel? As we have seen, the fundamental turning in the *Institutes* as a whole occurs with the inserted chapter vi of Book II, where Calvin insists that all that has gone before depends upon the coming of the Mediator, so that the equation Faith in Christ equals faith in God comes to the fore. Now a similar clarification is at hand, for only as this insight is taken within can it truly be ours. Notice the spiraling character of Calvin's system. Just as he had said in introducing chapter vi of Book II, so he must say here that all that has gone before depends upon what must be understood now:

> [e(a)]We must now examine this question. How do
> we receive those benefits which the Father be-
> stowed on his only-begotten Son—not for Christ's
> own private use, but that he might enrich poor and
> needy men? First, we must understand that as long
> as Christ remains outside of us, and we are
> separated from him, all that he has suffered and
> done for the salvation of the human race remains
> useless and of no value for us. (III.i.1 [537])

These opening lines of Book III are quickly linked to
the pervasive theme of Calvin's entire line of reflection, for it is only by way of the Spirit that this "taking
within" occurs:

> [e(a)]It is true that we obtain this by faith. Yet since
> we see that not all indiscriminately embrace that
> communion with Christ which is offered through
> the gospel, reason itself teaches us to climb higher
> and to examine into the secret energy of the Spirit,
> by which we come to enjoy Christ and all his
> benefits. (III.i.1 [537])

What is this "secret energy of the Spirit"? In
III.i.3, Calvin lists scriptural titles of the Holy Spirit.
Particularly arresting is his comment on Luke 3:16,
where *fire* and the Spirit are mentioned in the same
breath:

> [b(a)]Persistently boiling away and burning up our
> vicious and inordinate desires, he enflames our
> hearts with the love of God and with zealous
> devotion. (III.i.3 [540])

This calls to the mind of the editor the fact that
"Calvin's emblem of the flaming heart on an out-
stretched hand bore the motto: *'Cor meum quasi
immolatum tibi offero, Domine'* " (540 n.6). That we are

led to offer our flaming heart to God is the work of the Spirit within us. Hence, in the following paragraph Calvin insists that "faith is the principal work of the Holy Spirit" (III.i.4 [541]). He reads Ephesians 1:13 to indicate that

> [e]Paul shows the Spirit to be the inner teacher by whose effort the promise of salvation penetrates into our minds, a promise that would otherwise only strike the air or beat upon our ears. (III.i.4 [541])

In that "faith itself has no other source than the Spirit" he both can and will use precisely the same metaphor with reference to Christ:

> [e(b)]Paul so highly commends the "ministry of the Spirit" [II Cor. 3:6] for the reason that teachers would shout to no effect if Christ himself, inner Schoolmaster, did not by his Spirit draw to himself those given to him by the Father. . . . We have said that perfect salvation is found in the person of Christ. Accordingly, that we may become partakers of it "he baptizes us in the Holy Spirit and fire" . . . [Luke 3:16]. (III.i.4 [542])

Such, then, is the secret energy of the Spirit, and in the light of all of this Calvin turns to the discussion of that *true piety* first introduced at the outset of the *Institutes* in I.ii.1 (41). There, it will be recalled, Calvin delineated piety as "that reverence joined with love of God which the knowledge of his benefits induces" (I.ii.1 [41]). As we have seen, this knowledge of God's benefits is ours by way of faith in Christ (II.vi). Now Calvin focuses his understanding of this faith as the direct result of the witness of scripture:

> ᵇThis, then, is the true knowledge of Christ, if we receive him as he is offered by the Father: namely, ᵉ⁽ᵇ⁾clothed with his gospel. For just as he has been appointed as the goal of our faith, so we cannot take the right road to him unless the gospel goes before us. (III.ii.6 [548])

Calvin contends for "a permanent relationship between faith and the Word" (III.ii.6 [548]). And this leads him to offer, provisionally in a sense, a key definition:

> ᵇWe hold faith to be a knowledge of God's will toward us, perceived from his Word. (III.ii.6 [549])

That this is at best a provisional definition roots in the fact that by itself, so to say, the word is not enough:

> ᵇBut since man's heart is not aroused to faith at every word of God, we must find out at this point what, strictly speaking, faith looks to in the Word. (III.ii.7 [549-550])

Why, precisely, is it that not "every word of God" arouses faith? Calvin's answer is clear, and once again those who would adduce him for a blind and literalistic biblicism fail to grasp the depths of his claim. They simply have not read him with care:

> ᵇWhere our conscience sees only indignation and vengeance, how can it fail to tremble and be afraid? or to shun the God whom it dreads? Yet faith ought to seek God, not to shun him. (III.ii.7 [550])

The words that cause us to tremble and flee from God are not those which lead to faith! For, "merely to know something of God's will is not to be accounted faith" (III.ii.7 [550]). For

> [b]it is after we have learned that our salvation rests with God that we are attracted to seek him. (III.ii.7 [550])

Thus Calvin arrives at his basic delineation, and this is anything but provisional:

> [b]Now we shall possess a right definition of faith if we call it a firm and certain knowledge of God's benevolence toward us, founded upon the truth of the freely given promise in Christ, both revealed in our minds and sealed upon our hearts through the Holy Spirit. (III.ii.7 [551])

Note the fact that these lines originate with the 1539 edition of the *Institutes*. The control definition in I.ii.1 (41) was inserted in the 1559 edition. Here, then, is the line of reflection that informed it, and once again we are virtually inside Calvin's own mind, watching the *Institutes* unfold. This is one of those key junctures which demonstrate the *organismic* character of Calvin's thought. The reason that the delineation of *piety* at the outset of the *Institutes* keeps coming to mind as we read is that the argument of Book III does indeed inform the argument of the *Institutes* at large. The formulation now before us leads directly to a central contention informing the content of Book III as a whole, for the elaboration directly at hand links faith so understood with its result in the life of the believer:

> [a]Since faith embraces Christ, as offered to us by the Father [cf. John 6:29]—that is, since he is offered not [b(a)]only for righteousness, forgiveness of sins,

> and peace, but also for sanctification [cf. 1 Cor.
> 1:30] and the fountain of the water of life [John
> 7:38; cf. 4:14]—without a doubt, no one can duly
> know him without at the same time apprehending
> the sanctification of the Spirit. bOr, if anyone
> desires some plainer statement, faith rests upon
> the knowledge of Christ. And Christ cannot be
> known apart from the sanctification of his Spirit. It
> follows that faith can in no wise be separated from
> a devout disposition. (III.ii.8 [552–553])

The phrase "from a devout disposition" translates *a
pio affectu* (*OS* 4:18). The Latin almost defies translation, but do recall the formulation at the outset of the
Institutes, to which we have been making such
frequent reference:

> eI call "piety" that reverence joined with love of
> God which the knowledge of his benefits induces.
> (I.ii.1 [41])

This is the *mode of becoming* which characterizes the
life of the believer. Thus I would read Calvin to say
that since Christ cannot be known "apart from the
sanctification of his Spirit," it is clear that faith cannot
be separated from that *mode of becoming which true piety
embodies*.

A memorable recasting of this very point is
worthy of close attention. In the opening lines of
paragraph 14 of this same chapter Calvin notes the
interrelationship between faith and knowledge, insisting that the latter receives decisive reformulation
at the hands of faith itself:

> bNow let us examine anew the individual parts of
> the definition of faith. After we have diligently

> examined it no doubt, I believe, will remain. When
> we call faith "knowledge" we do not mean
> comprehension of the sort that is commonly
> concerned with those things which fall under
> human sense perception. For faith is so far above
> sense that man's mind has to go beyond and rise
> above itself in order to attain it. (III.ii.14 [559])

A noticeably Hebraic understanding of "knowing" as "relationship" is in operation here, and it
leads Calvin to a choice formulation, at the outset of
paragraph 16:

> bHere, indeed, is the chief hinge on which faith
> turns: that we do not regard the promises of mercy
> that God offers as true only outside ourselves, but
> not at all in us; rather that we make them ours by
> inwardly embracing them. Hence, at last is born
> that confidence which Paul elsewhere calls
> "peace" [Rom. 5:1], unless someone may prefer to
> derive peace from it. Now it is an assurance that
> renders the conscience calm and peaceful before
> God's judgment. Without it the conscience must be
> harried by disturbed alarm, and almost torn to
> pieces; unless perhaps, forgetting God and self, it
> for the moment sleeps. (III.ii.16 [561])

Ponder at length the momentous claim here
made, and note how it bears so heavily on the
mistaken assumption that Calvin's ethic was informed by frightful austerity. The rigorous character
of life in the Spirit, which we are about to examine, is
a function of the already delivered conscience. It has
nothing to do with the dreadful fear of a stumbling
perfectionism. Nor can it lend itself to the kind of
reflection of some on this side of Freud, viz., the claim

that the only thing to do with the conscience is to anesthetize it. Why? One of the truly memorable sets of lines in Book III contains Calvin's answer:

> bIt now remains to pour into the heart itself what the mind has absorbed. For the Word of God is not received by faith if it flits about in the top of the brain, but when it takes root in the depth of the heart that it may be an invincible defense to withstand and drive off all the stratagems of temptation. (III.ii.36 [583])

How do we detect the presence of a hearing of the word of God that moves from the brain to the heart? This leads us to the ninth parameter.

IX. Accordingly, the result of faith must be treated before the doctrine of justification by faith, if the latter is to be properly understood.

Our ninth parameter focuses the heart of Calvin's ethic. We are at the very nerve center of the argument of Book III, and this contention turns on a decisive structural maneuver, one that must be placed alongside other such operations that disclose the inner workings of the faithful mind of this systematician. A crucial insight is here manifest: Whenever a careful thinker must choose between two points that equally demand attention, note well which is given initial attention and why this is the case. We have already noted Calvin's contention that faith, knowledge, and sanctification must be understood together (see III.ii.8). Now, in the form of understanding the relationship between *repentance* and *reconciliation*, Calvin places *sanctification* in the controlling position. For him, the *consequence* of faith is the clue to the *significance* of faith:

> [e]With good reason, the sum of the gospel is held to consist in repentance and forgiveness of sins [Luke 24:47; Acts 5:31]. Any discussion of faith, therefore, that omitted these two topics would be barren and mutilated and well-nigh useless. Now, both repentance and forgiveness of sins—that is, newness of life and free reconciliation—are conferred on us by Christ, and both are attained by us through faith. As a consequence, reason and the order of teaching demand that I begin to discuss both at this point. [e(b)]However, our immediate transition will be from faith to repentance. [e]For when this topic is rightly understood it will better appear how man is justified by faith alone, and simple pardon; nevertheless actual holiness of life, so to speak, is not separated from free imputation of righteousness. (III.iii.1 [592–593])

On this basis Calvin explicitly equates repentance with regeneration. Repentance is a process, and he moves with careful precision to establish this:

> [b]The Hebrew word for "repentance" is derived from conversion [e]or return; [b]the Greek word, from change of mind or of intention. And the thing itself corresponds closely to the etymology of both words. The meaning is that, departing from ourselves, we turn to God, and having taken off our former mind, we put on a new. [b(a)]On this account, in my judgment, repentance can thus be well defined: it is the true turning of our life to God, a turning that arises from a pure and earnest fear of him; and it consists in the mortification of our flesh and of the old man, and in the vivification of the Spirit. (III.iii.5 [597])

This involves nothing less than the *restoration* of humanity to the realization of the intention of ultimacy. Since such an astonishing transformation is at hand, the progress toward its fulfillment is *necessarily slow:*

> bIn a word, I interpret repentance as regeneration, whose sole end is to restore in us the image of God that had been disfigured and all but obliterated through Adam's transgression. . . . eAnd indeed, this restoration does not take place in one moment or one day or one year; but through continual and sometimes even slow advances God wipes out in his elect the corruptions of the flesh, cleanses them of guilt, consecrates them to himself as temples renewing all their minds to true purity that they may practice repentance throughout their lives and know that this warfare will end only at death. (III.iii.9 [601])

So it is that the subject of "the Christian life" comes into view.

X. The Christian life has to do with believers' faithful response to the redeeming act of God.

If the ninth parameter focuses the heart of Calvin's ethic, the tenth indicates its goal and shape. The goal is clear: we are to respond to God's redemptive act with redeemed acts of our own:

> eThe object of regeneration, as we have said, is to manifest in the life of believers a harmony and agreement between God's righteousness and their obedience, and thus to confirm the adoption that they have received as sons. (III.vi.1 [684])

Note well the relational character of the insight at hand. A harmony and agreement (*symmetria et consensus* [*OS* 4:146]) between God's act and our own—this is what we are to strive for as we act out our redemption. And this *acting out of our redemption* is the confirmation of our redemption. We are adopted as God's own children. The life we are given to live is to be a life of response to what has already occurred. So Calvin introduces his attempt to delineate "from various passages of Scripture a pattern for the conduct of life *in order that those who heartily repent may not err in their zeal*" (III.vi.1 [684]).

It is entirely in order to add our own emphasis to these words. The issue is *qualitative, not quantitative:*

> [b]I do not intend to develop, here, the instruction in living that I am now about to offer to the point of describing individual virtues at length, and of digressing into exhortations. Such may be sought from others' writings, especially from the homilies of the fathers. To show the godly man how he may be directed to a rightly ordered life, and briefly to set down some universal rule with which to determine his duties—this will be quite enough for me. (III.vi.1 [685])

But this kind of qualitative demand has its quantitative side. In a manner very much in line with what we have already seen regarding Calvin's understanding of the third use of the law, the demand at hand is intensely affirmative in character. The quantitative side of this qualitative demand has to do with the fact that the astonishing possibility that is ours—truly responding to God with confirming acts of our own—can be distorted by the very zeal it

generates. The redeemed life must adhere to norms;
otherwise it will wander into aberration:

> bNow this Scriptural instruction of which we speak
> has two main aspects. The first is that the love of
> righteousness, to which we are otherwise not at all
> inclined by nature, may be instilled and estab-
> lished in our hearts; the second, that a rule be set
> forth for us that does not let us wander about in our
> zeal for righteousness. (III.vi.2 [685])

Thus we are to study diligently the righteousness
which it is our privilege to attempt. And if our lives do
indeed demonstrate the contours of redemption,
the gestalt of adoption, what we realize in action is
that very piety which Calvin understood to be
intrinsic to recognizing the *benefits* of the knowledge of God (see yet again I.ii.1 [41]). To this end
there are two very basic components of Calvin's
thought that must always be remembered. The
first has to do with our limit, the second with our
steadfast self-understanding.

In our zeal for righteousness we must always
reckon with the enemy of integrity, perfectionism.
The process of responding to God's act with acts of
our own is intractably slow:

> bI do not insist that the moral life of a Christian
> man breathe nothing but the very gospel, yet this
> ought to be desired, and we must strive toward it.
> But I do not so strictly demand evangelical
> perfection that I would not acknowledge as a
> Christian one who has not yet attained it. For thus
> all would be excluded from the church, since no
> one is found who is not far removed from it, while
> many have advanced a little toward it whom it

would nevertheless be unjust to cast away. (III.vi.5 [688])

The austerity so often ascribed to Calvin withers before passages such as these. The true bases of his ethical insight are all too often overlooked. It is, as he insists, a "target . . . set before our eyes," toward which we are "earnestly to aim," and only so will we achieve "the opposite of a double heart" (III.vi.5 [688]).

> bLet each one of us, then, proceed according to the measure of his puny capacity and set out upon the journey we have begun. . . . And let us not despair at the slightness of our success; for even though attainment may not correspond to desire, when today outstrips yesterday the effort is not lost. Only let us look toward our mark with sincere simplicity and aspire to our goal; not fondly flattering ourselves, nor excusing our own evil deeds, but with continuous effort striving toward this end: that we may surpass ourselves in goodness until we attain to goodness itself. (III.vi.5 [689])

All that Calvin has to say in these memorable chapters now unfolds in the light of Romans 12:1. Nothing less than the presentation of our bodily existence as the living sacrifice of which Paul spoke can constitute our true and worshipful response to God. Truly it is Calvin the preacher who announces his great theme:

> bNow the great thing is this: we are consecrated and dedicated to God in order that we may thereafter think, speak, meditate, and do, nothing except to his glory. (III.vii.1 [690])

His elaboration of this is one of the truly lyrical passages of the *Institutes:*

> [b]We are not our own: let not our reason nor our will, therefore, sway our plans and deeds. We are not our own: let us therefore not set it as our goal to seek what is expedient for us according to the flesh. We are not our own: in so far as we can, let us therefore forget ourselves and all that is ours.
>
> Conversely, we are God's: let us therefore live for him and die for him. We are God's: let his wisdom and will therefore rule all our actions. We are God's: let all the parts of our life accordingly strive toward him as our only lawful goal [Rom. 14:8; cf. 1 Cor. 6:19]. O, how much has that man profited who, having been taught that he is not his own, has taken away dominion and rule from his own reason that he may yield it to God! For, as consulting our self-interest is the pestilence that most effectively leads to our destruction, so the sole haven of salvation is to be wise in nothing and to will nothing through ourselves but to follow the leading of the Lord alone. (III.vii.1 [690])

That we are in the presence of memorable chapters indeed has a striking corroboration. In 1550 the five chapters beginning with chapter vi of Book III were published separately as *The Golden Booklet of the Christian Life* (see p. 1x n. 65), and in the preceding year, 1549, these chapters were the first section of the *Institutes* to be translated into English, as *The Life and Communicacion of a Christen Man* (see p. xlii n. 19). We have already taken note that Calvin deliberately treated the subject matter of sanctification before taking up the issue of understanding justification by faith (in discussing III.iii.1 within the framework of the ninth parameter). How far was he willing to press this point? As far as insisting on what we have just heard, as the necessary introduction to a true account of the depths of our justification by faith alone. Such is the far-reaching significance of the fact that whereas Calvin shared with Luther the first two uses of the law, it was his own third use that indicated the astonishing possibility of the ethic of response at the heart of Book III of the *Institutes*.

XI. All this turns on justification by faith, and hence the understanding of Christian freedom.

Now the doctrine of justification by faith can be discussed. Calvin has carefully prepared the way for his version of this central emphasis of Reformation thought. He makes common cause with Luther in emphasizing the centrality of the doctrine of justification by faith. But, as we have seen him go to great lengths to explain, this must not be discussed in isolation from its yield. So to move is to misunderstand grace. It is not based on human merit, and thus it is not the result of human action in any sense. But it does yield the work of redeemed humanity, which is offered the astonishing possibility of responding to God's acts with acts of its own.

Thus Calvin commences his discussion of justification with a recapitulation of the issue at hand:

> bChrist was given to us by God's generosity, to be grasped and possessed by us in faith. By partaking of him, we principally receive a double grace: namely, that being reconciled to God through Christ's blamelessness, we may have in heaven

> instead of a Judge a gracious Father; and secondly,
> that sanctified by Christ's spirit we may cultivate
> blamelessness and purity of life. Of regeneration,
> indeed, the second of these gifts, I have said what
> seemed sufficient. The theme of justification was
> therefore more lightly touched upon because it was
> more to the point to understand first how little
> devoid of good works is the faith, through which
> alone we obtain free righteousness by the mercy of
> God; and what is the nature of the good works of
> the saints, with which part of this question is
> concerned. (III.xi.1 [725–726])

Once all of this has been explored, it is impossible
to overstate the significance of the doctrine of
justification, and once this has been clarified, it is not
dangerous so to do:

> bWe must now discuss these matters thoroughly.
> And we must so discuss them as to bear in mind
> that this is the main hinge on which religion turns.
> (III.xi.1 [726])

In the light of his delineation of the Christian life,
and consistent with his insistence on the fact that the
third use of the law discloses its true significance,
Calvin emphasizes the *experiential* character of justification.

> bThis is the experience of faith through which the
> sinner comes into possession of his salvation when
> from the teaching of the gospel he acknowledges
> that he has been reconciled to God: that with
> Christ's righteousness interceding and forgiveness
> of sins accomplished he is justified. And although
> regenerated by the Spirit of God, he ponders the
> everlasting righteousness laid up for him not in the

> good works to which he inclines but in the sole
> righteousness of Christ. (III.xi.16 [746])

We must linger with this passage and the insight
to which it leads. There is no doubt that justification
yields the inclination to work out its result. There is
equally no doubt that the latter effort corroborates,
but does not establish, justification. Why? The base of
this new inclination is a new relationship, that
between faith and the gospel, and hence the relationship between God and humanity:

> bHere we should recall to mind the relation that we
> have previously established between faith and the
> gospel. For faith is said to justify because it receives
> and embraces the righteousness offered in the
> gospel. (III.xi.17 [746])

This new relationship generates the possibility of
new relationships; the latter are the result, not the
basis, of the former. Hence Luther was right. It is a
matter of justification by faith *alone*.

> bNow the reader sees how fairly the Sophists today
> cavil against our doctrine when we say that man is
> justified by faith alone. . . . If righteousness is
> revealed in the gospel, surely no mutilated or half
> righteousness but a full and perfect righteousness
> is contained there. The law therefore has no place
> in it. (III.xi.19 [748–749])

Calvin's version of the *sola fide* is emphatic and
unequivocal. That he felt he must treat the issue with
the massive care we have been attending to in some
detail, and thus that he was profoundly committed to
moving beyond Luther's formulation of this central

insistence, did not diminish his fundamental agreement on the basic contention. This was controversial and he knew it: "Calvin, in defending *sola fide*, is aware that numerous attacks have been made on it, and that it has been roundly condemned by the Council of Trent" (748 n. 35). The controversy is necessary, for nothing less than the heart of the gospel is at stake. He meant it when we heard him say that we are looking at "the main hinge on which religion turns" (III.xi.1 [726]).

One can hardly hear all of this without thinking yet again of the definition of true piety at the outset of the *Institutes*. That "reverence joined with love of God" which constitutes true piety turns on the *knowledge of God's benefits*. Justification by faith is at the center of the gospel because it discloses the inexhaustible depths of these gifts—Christian freedom. Like Luther before him, Calvin treats freedom as the heart of the matter. For him, this is the case because it discloses justification's *power:*

> [a]We must now discuss Christian freedom. He who proposes to summarize gospel teaching ought by no means to omit an explanation of this topic. For it is a thing of prime necessity, and apart from a knowledge of it consciences dare undertake almost nothing without doubting; they hesitate and recoil from many things; they constantly waver and are afraid. [e]But freedom is especially an appendage of justification and is of no little avail in understanding its power. (III.xix.1 [833])

The passage before us contains an emphasis present in Calvin's thought from the 1536 edition of the *Institutes* forward. The last sentence was added in

1559. The longer Calvin reflected on all of this, the more he came to understand that justification has its central significance in freeing the conscience from the paralysis of guilt. The reason that the discussion of Christian freedom is a matter of "prime necessity" is that it is the locus of faithful experience. We have heard him set out his remarkable grasp of Christian life. Now we behold his understanding of what makes it possible.

Calvin treated Christian freedom under three headings. First:

> [a]The consciences of believers, in seeking assurance of their justification before God, should rise above and advance beyond the law, forgetting all law righteousness. (III.xix.2 [834])

A second step is the direct implication of this, and it is reminiscent of the entire argument concerning the third use of the law in Book II:

> [a]The second part, dependent upon the first, is that consciences observe the law, not as if constrained by the necessity of the law, but that freed from the law's yoke they willingly obey God's will. (III.xix.4 [836])

The third move is the choice one, and it contains his memorable observations concerning the "adiaphora," the realm of indifferent things:

> [a]The third part of Christian freedom lies in this: regarding outward things that are of themselves "indifferent," we are not bound before God by any religious obligation preventing us from sometimes using them and other times not using them, indifferently. (III.xix.7 [838])

The elaboration of this point gives the lie to the one sense in which the term "indifferent" can be misleading. The issue is hardly marginal, and it rings true to what we have already heard Calvin say in opposing perfectionism as inimical to the Christian life:

> aBut these matters are more important than is commonly believed. For when consciences once ensnare themselves, they enter a long and inextricable maze, not easy to get out of. If a man begins to doubt whether he may use linen for sheets, shirts, handkerchiefs, and napkins, he will afterward be uncertain also about hemp; finally, doubt will even arise over tow. For he will turn over in his mind whether he can sup without napkins, or go without a handkerchief. If any man should consider daintier food unlawful, in the end he will not be at peace before God, when he eats either black bread or common victuals, while it occurs to him that he could sustain his body on even coarser foods. If he boggles at sweet wine, he will not with clear conscience drink even flat wine, and finally he will not dare touch water if sweeter and cleaner than other water. To sum up, he will come to the point of considering it wrong to step upon a straw across his path, as the saying goes. (III.xix.7 [839])

That these are probably surprising words to be found in Calvin's *Institutes* bears witness that many persons who appeal to his thought do not serve him well. Again, the prevailing assumption regarding Calvin's austerity must be in full retreat. More than that, though, the issue at hand turns on the question concerning doubt as the inevitable companion of the compulsive, driven conscience. Justification delivers us from this.

How do we realize this deliverance? I am convinced that it is no accident that Calvin's great chapter on Christian freedom is followed by his equally memorable chapter on prayer. It is instructive to note his title for chapter xx of Book III: "Prayer, Which Is the Chief Exercise of Faith, and by Which We Daily Receive God's Benefits." This calls to mind immediately the delineation of true piety in I.ii.1, which we have had occasion so often to ponder. And given the organismic character of the argument of the *Institutes*—given, that is, the fact that all of these parameters are constantly operative in an intertwined way—it is hardly wide of the mark to claim that piety itself is a decisive aspect of Christian freedom. In that so much is made of "spirituality" these days, it is important to insist that freedom, deliverance from the troubled conscience, and the continual, daily receiving of God's benefits—all of these animate Calvin's remarkable understanding of prayer:

> bIt is . . . by the benefit of prayer that we reach those riches which are laid up for us with the Heavenly Father. (III.xx.2 [851])

This having been said, the first item of business for Calvin is the dismissal of a decisive misleading contention:

> bBut, someone will say, does God not know, even without being reminded, both in what respect we are troubled and what is expedient for us, so that it may seem in a sense superfluous that he should be stirred up by our prayers—as if he were drowsily blinking or even sleeping until he is aroused by our voice? (III.xx.3 [851–852])

Prayer is not superfluous for Calvin—he can think of six reasons why this is the case. The passage is long, and it must be read slowly, for its cumulative impact is the decisive point to this line of reflection. Note that Calvin was constantly revising this extended formulation. Watch for three emphases: that prayer is the channel for our realization of God's benefits, that what is at stake is nothing less than the confirmation of God's providence, and that the reality of God's presence, which we practice in prayer, transcends words:

> bTherefore, even though, while we grow dull and stupid toward our miseries, he watches and keeps guard on our behalf, and sometimes even helps us unasked, still it is very important for us to call upon him: First, that our hearts may be fired with a zealous and burning desire ever to seek, love, and serve him, while we become accustomed in every need to flee to him as to a sacred anchor. Secondly, that there may enter our hearts no desire and no wish at all of which we should be ashamed to make him a witness, while we learn to set all our wishes before his eyes, and even to pour out our whole hearts. Thirdly, that we be prepared to receive his benefits with true gratitude of heart and thanksgiving, benefits that our prayer reminds us come from his hand [cf.Ps.145:15-16]. Fourthly, moreover, that, having obtained what we were seeking, and being convinced that he has answered our prayers, we should be led to meditate upon his kindness more ardently. And fifthly, that at the same time we embrace with greater delight those things which we acknowledge to have been obtained by prayers. Finally, that e(b)use and experience may, according to the measure of our feebleness, confirm bhis e(b)providence, bwhile we understand not

> only that he promises never to fail us, and of his own will opens the way to call upon him at the very point of necessity, [e] but also that he ever extends his hand to help his own, not wet-nursing them with words [*"Nec lactare eos verbis"* (852 n. 4)] but defending them with present help. (III.xx.3 [852])

Here the presence of God transcends even the lisping God we encountered in I.xiii.1, when we first wrestled with God's accommodation to us, for we are at the very depths of the practice of the presence of ultimacy in our lives.

How is this practice ordered? Calvin sets out *four rules*. The first demands an attitude worthy of what prayer intends to effect:

> [a]Now for framing prayer duly and properly, let this be the first rule: [b]that we be disposed in mind and heart as befits those who enter conversation with God. (III.xx.4 [853])

This initial demand implies a second one—the constant recognition of our limits:

> [e(b/a)]Let this be the second rule: that in our petitions we ever sense our own insufficiency, and earnestly pondering how we need all that we seek, join with this prayer an earnest—nay, burning—desire to attain it. (III.xx.6 [856])

Clearly the integrity of prayer is at stake in this second rule—there may be no double-talk, no superficiality where true prayer is attempted. For the practice of the presence of God is awesome, or it is sheer fraud. Hence the warning of the third rule:

> [e(a)]To this let us join a third rule: that anyone who stands before God to pray, in his humility giving

> glory completely to God, abandon all thought of
> his own glory, cast off all notion of his own worth,
> in fine, put away all self-assurance—ᵇlest if we
> claim for ourselves anything, even the least bit, we
> should become vainly puffed up, and perish at his
> presence. (III.xx.8 [859])

But this stern warning gives way to the abiding
confidence that the presence of the God in whom we
believe yields unending hope:

> ᵉThe fourth rule is that, ᵇthus cast down and
> overcome by true humility, we should be nonethe-
> less encouraged to pray by a sure hope that our
> prayer will be answered. (III.xx.11 [862])

Since, that is, it is the God we know in the Mediator,
Jesus the Christ, who is present, to pray is itself the
answer to prayer.

The trouble with rules as clearly stated as these is
that they are likely to be absolutized. This is why it is
crucial to insist that for Calvin prayer is the exercise of
Christian freedom. Thus before he leaves these rules
he relaxes them:

> ᵉThis also is worth noting: what I have set forth on
> the four rules of right praying is not so rigorously
> required that God will reject those prayers in
> which he finds neither perfect faith nor repent-
> ance, together with a warmth of zeal and petitions
> rightly conceived. (III.xx.16 [872])

Thus it is the intentionality pervading these rules that
is critically significant for us, and it is in the same
mode that the marvelous exposition of the Lord's
Prayer, with which the chapter culminates, unfolds

step by step. Note especially the fact that this is a prayer that *we* pray:

> ªThese . . . petitions, in which we especially commend to God ourselves and all our possessions, clearly show what we have previously said: that the prayers of Christians ought to be public, and to look to the public edification of the church and the advancement of the believers' fellowship. For each man does not pray that something be given to him privately, but all of us in common ask our bread, forgiveness of sins, not to be led into temptation, and to be freed from evil. (III.xx.47 [915])

Note also that the Lord's Prayer will always be our abiding model, not in a literalistic sense, but rather in the sense that

> ªwe mean only this: that no man should ask for, expect, or demand, anything at all except what is included, by way of summary, in this prayer; and though the words may be utterly different, yet the sense ought not to vary. (III.xx.49 [917])

To contemplate at depth the petitions of the Lord's Prayer is to know what Calvin knows:

> ªHere nothing is left out that ought to be thought of in the praises of God, nothing that ought to come into man's mind for his own welfare. And, indeed, it is so precisely framed that hope of attempting anything better is rightly taken away from all men. To sum up, let us remember that this is the teaching of Divine Wisdom, teaching what it willed and willing what was needful. (III.xx.49 [917])

Only if the progression from freedom to prayer is in mind will we grasp what Calvin, as of the 1559 edition of the *Institutes*, seeks to clarify in the doctrine of election. Strange it is that, given the progression of his argument, this has been so often overlooked.

XII. Election (predestination) must be understood in the context of the experience of the Christian life.

None of the changes that Calvin made in working out the 1559 edition of the *Institutes* is more important than the others, for they all reflect the same creativity at work, and it is this creativity we seek to bring forward into today's reflection. What is going on here, however, demands prolonged attention. The fact is that the primary emphasis of the subsequent tradition does not take it into account, and this single fact more than any other accounts for the prevailing view of Calvin's austere, unyielding devotion to the total depravity of humanity, overcome for some but not for all the rest by God's remote, inscrutable decree of limited favor for the chosen few. In the light of Calvin's final writing on this matter this is *not* where he himself finally came down, and it most decidedly is not where the significance of his thought for our reflection now comes into sharp focus.

The basic point which we must explore in depth is succinctly stated by the editors of our edition in the initial footnote that introduces chapter xxi: "While predestination is much stressed by Calvin, the formal treatment of the topic falls under the head not of the doctrine of God but of the doctrine of salvation." Included in this extensive note is the fascinating observation that this culminating maneuver of

Calvin's reflection had precedents (though to my knowledge he did not take this into account): "His position had, in fact, been in the main anticipated in the writings of medieval Augustinians, especially those of the fourteenth century, such as Thomas Bradwardine and Gregory of Rimini" (920 n.1).

That this is the culminating maneuver in Calvin's thought on election is also indicated by our editors, with an incisive alert in the initial note that introduces Book I's chapter xvi on providence:

> In editions 1539–1554, Calvin treated the topics of providence and predestination in the same chapter. In the final edition they are widely separated, providence being set here in the context of the knowledge of God the Creator, while predestination is postponed to III.xxi–xxiv, where it comes within the general treatment of the redemptive work of the Holy Spirit. (197 n.1)

Why this move? The answer to this question is clearly implied by the new location of the discussion, viz., election and predestination (in fact, the terms are identical) must be understood within the context of the living of the Christian life. That is to say, the issue turns on Christian experience. As we shall see, the fact is that this implication has a double significance. First, it is explicitly indicated in an impressive number of passages. Second, Calvin's final discussion of the matter contains unfinished business, for he did not complete the process of thinking through the meaning of this new location of the doctrine in the sweep of the argument of the *Institutes* as a whole.

A further specification is in order as we move into pondering the passages now before us, and it must be formulated since it is intrinsic to the purpose of our present investigation. Throughout the preceding editions of the *Institutes* Calvin had linked providence and predestination, discussing this linkage within the context of elaborating the understanding of God the Creator. In this context election will be understood almost exclusively as a function of the *power* of God. That Calvin was willing to leave matters there for most of his life is obvious, even though much of the treatment of election contained a countervailing emphasis. Moreover, in that providence and election were treated together, and given the fact that election and predestination are terms that virtually stand in apposition, the understanding of providence itself is thrown into a chronological mode to such a degree that the *remoteness* of the powerful God who predestines some to salvation and the rest to damnation yields the heavily deterministic ring to each of the terms "providence" and "predestination" whenever and wherever they strike modern ears.

Now it would seem to be the case that for Calvin, as well as for the preponderance of the tradition before him, including no less a figure than Augustine himself, the notion of the power of God is so intrinsic to the doctrine of God at large that if it is relaxed in any way whatsoever, faith is fatally wounded. Thus the gospel itself turns on the decisive contention that the powerful God is loving, a contention that is good news indeed, as long as one is certain that he or she is among the elect. Oversimplified though that may be, it is clear in our time and place that the only case for belief in God pivots on the *love* of God, not on the power of God, and the question for us is thus the reverse of the old one. For us the gospel is that the loving God is powerful, and this indeed is good news. It would be utterly wrong to claim that the same was unequivocally the case for Calvin. But it is irresponsible to overlook the fact that his own nervous creativity was driving him in this direction.

This is the decisive significance of his 1559 move. Election is separated from providence and creation and moved far down into the depths of the unfolding expositions of the *Institutes*. In fact, it is not just an implication of Christology for him now, it is part and parcel of the treatment of God in the present tense, the discussion, that is, of God the Holy Spirit, and hence the treatment of the experience of the Christian life. This is why the remarkable christological insertion in the new chapter vi of Book II is so widely separated from the treatment now at hand. Experience had to be put in place *first*. Only then should predestination be discussed. And this necessitated treatments of the third use of the law, the threefold office of Christ, the fact that sanctification must be discussed *before* justification, the outline of the ethic of response, and the true depths of prayer, prior to the exploration of the central mystery of God's love, the doctrine of election. Only a holistic reading of the *Institutes* can disclose this. Such a conclusion can be reached only when the full sweep of the argument is in view. The surprising yield of such a discipline is the fact that Calvin is a worthy companion as we search in our own time for the understanding that faith brings when this matter is properly approached.

The intensely positive point we must see first begins with a disclaimer. Surprisingly enough, and

from the 1539 edition of the *Institutes* forward, the
central polarity with which Calvin is concerned is not
that between salvation and damnation. The point of
departure of chapter xxi reads

> bIn actual fact, the covenant of life is not preached
> equally among all men, and among those to whom
> it is preached, it does not gain the same acceptance
> either constantly or in equal degree. In this
> diversity the wonderful depth of God's judgment
> is made known. (III.xxi.1 [920–921])

Reflected here is the experience that every
preacher knows, and that in a double sense. Both
as hearer and as proclaimer, one who is gripped by
the gospel will be dismayed that others are unmoved,
that all are not responsive. But the antidote to despair
over this impasse is to regard it as illustrative of the
awesome depth of God's judgment. How so?

> eWe shall never be clearly persuaded, as we ought
> to be, that our salvation flows from the wellspring
> of God's free mercy until we come to know his
> eternal election, which illumines God's grace by
> this contrast: that he does not indiscriminately
> adopt all into the hope of salvation but gives to
> some what he denies to others. (III.xxi.1 [921])

The contrast is earthbound. Clearly, not all have
the *hope of salvation,* and those who do have it solely by
way of the grace of God. But note the contrast. It is not
between the *presence* of salvation and the *presence* of
damnation. It is between the presence of the hope of
salvation and its absence. That this particular absence
means damnation for Calvin is obvious. That it may or
may not for us is possible. The fact of the matter,

however, is this. The *explicit* contrast that Calvin sets out to explore transcends his time and lands in our time. Christian experience today also knows the mystification intrinsic to the proclamation of the gospel. Why is it that what is so moving, so redemptive, so transforming, for one is devoid of significance for another? What struggles for expression here is simply this: the doctrine of election has to do with the self-understanding of those who hear the gospel. It is a doctrine of redemption. The doctrine of election does not have to do with the self-understanding of the rejected. It even treads on shaky ground in using that term. What is missing for those who do not hear the gospel is the hope of salvation. Not to have that hope is indeed a damned shame. But it may not be shameful damnation. Calvin did not get that far. But he could have. We may be reluctant to go that far. But we may have to, given the astonishing claim of the very gospel the elect hear.

If the doctrine of election has to do with the self-understanding of those who hear the gospel, what does this set of insights entail? Here Calvin is indeed clear. The *signs* of election are profoundly experiential. For those who do receive the gospel as good news have a sense of *calling* and know the great benefit that God has given (the very benefit that induces true piety [see I.ii.1 [41]]), the certainty, that is, of *justification*. Here, and here alone, the question of election and the *individual believer* can be addressed with assurance:

> [e]Although it is now sufficiently clear that God by his secret plan freely chooses whom he pleases, rejecting others, still his free election has been only

> half explained until we come to individual persons, to whom God not only offers salvation but so assigns it that the certainty of its effect is not in suspense or doubt. (III.xxi.7 [930])

Let there be no doubt that this formulation can be read with "double predestination eyes." But is that really to read what Calvin is most concerned to clarify? The subject he wishes to address with conviction has to do with the removal of *suspense* and *doubt*. Against these twin deceivers Calvin marshals the believer's calling as a "testimony of election" and the summons into freedom that justification brings as a "sign of its manifestation":

> bAs Scripture, then, clearly shows, we say that God once established by his eternal and unchangeable plan those whom he long before determined once for all to receive into salvation, and those whom, on the other hand, he would devote to destruction. e(b)We assert that, with respect to the elect, this plan was founded upon his freely given mercy, without regard to human worth; but by his just and irreprehensible but incomprehensible judgment bhe has barred the door of life to those whom he has given over to damnation. Now among the elect we regard the call as a testimony of election. Then we hold justification another sign of its manifestation. (III.xxi.7 [931])

Left in the realm of incomprehensibility is the question of the rejected. The only clarity on which we may dwell is the genuinely comprehendable character of the grace given to us. Summoned by justification into the freedom of faith, we are called to proclaim the gospel to all who would hear.

Once again, let there be no misunderstanding. The language of double predestination remains pervasively present in Calvin's discussion—inexorably so, from 1536 to 1554, where election was continually treated in close juxtaposition with the providence of God. At the same time, let there be no reluctance to discern that this language is now an intrusion into Calvin's discussion. This was simply beyond his horizon. But it most assuredly is not beyond ours. We too know the real base of the point at hand. It is the experience of believers. The real mystification will always remain. Why is that which is ultimate for them insignificant for others?

> [e(b)]Many persons dispute all these positions which we have set forth, especially the free election of believers; nevertheless, this cannot be shaken. . . . [e]Because God chooses some, and passes over others according to his own decision, they bring an action against him. But if the fact itself is well known, what will it profit them to quarrel against God? We teach nothing not borne out by experience: that God has always been free to bestow his grace on whom he wills. (III.xxii.1 [932])

Note well: the fact that is well known is experiential in character. Every preacher knows it. Not everyone hears the gospel. If those who hear it do so by the grace of God, then the real mystery is all the more intense. Why is it that some do not have this grace?

The bottom line of Calvin's thought on this question turns on an insight that will always be present when the gospel is truly heard. Election is a function of the freedom of God:

> eTo sum up: by free adoption God makes those
> whom he wills to be his sons; the intrinsic cause of
> this is in himself, for he is content with his own
> secret good pleasure. (III.xxii.7 [941])

Calvin both can and does adduce Ambrose, Origen,
Jerome, and Augustine in support of his interpretation
of scripture in elaborating this. He is willing, though, to
argue that they are not needed, since the issue is
intrinsic in justification itself. If merit were at stake,
God would have no choice but to redeem the worthy.
But works are not at the fulcrum of this ultimate
decision. Mercy alone is:

> bBut come now, let us imagine that these fathers
> are silent; let us pay attention to the matter itself. A
> difficult question was raised: whether God acted
> righteously in vouchsafing his grace to certain
> men. Paul could have settled this in one word, by
> proposing a regard for works. Why, then, does he
> not do this but rather continues a discourse that is
> fraught with the same difficulty? Why but because
> he ought not? For the Holy Spirit, speaking
> through his mouth, did not suffer from the fault of
> forgetfulness. Therefore he answers without cir-
> cumlocutions: God shows favor to his elect because
> he so wills; he has mercy upon them because he so
> wills. Accordingly, that declaration prevails: "I will
> show mercy on whom I will show mercy, and I will
> take pity on whom I will take pity" [Ex. 33:19 p.],
> as if he said: "God is moved to mercy for no other
> reason but that he wills to be merciful." Then that
> saying of Augustine remains true: "God's grace
> does not find but makes those fit to be chosen."
> (III.xxii.8 [942–943])

Calvin quotes Exodus from memory here, and, as
we have seen, such misquotations are invaluable

commentaries. In this case his understanding of the basic point in Paul's thought, in the light of which the misquote is in order, is itself exactingly precise. The elect do not merit grace, they receive it and are transformed by it, as Augustine claimed.

Love, not power; mercy, not tyranny—these are the marks of true insight into the gospel. How Calvin struggles to maintain the singularity of this claim! He will argue from the will of God in all that he says and thus claim that righteousness is simply what God wills, so that whatever God wills is right. Beyond this we may not go:

> [b]For his will is, and rightly ought to be, the cause of all things that are. For if it has any cause, something must precede it, to which it is, as it were, bound; this is unlawful to imagine. For God's will is so much the highest rule of righteousness that whatever he wills, by the very fact that he wills it, must be considered righteous. When, therefore, one asks why God has so done, we must reply: because he has willed it. But if you proceed further to ask why he so willed, you are seeking something greater and higher than God's will, which cannot be found. (III.xxiii.2 [949])

Having said this, Calvin immediately set in place two decisive qualifications. Neither *absolute might* nor *tyranny* may be taken as the implication of arguing that whatever God wills is righteous:

> [e]We do not advocate the fiction of "absolute might"; because this is profane, it ought rightly to be hateful to us. We fancy no lawless god who is a law unto himself. (III.xxiii.2 [950])

If the notion of absolute might is profane, that of tyranny is even worse, for it is profoundly misleading:

> [b]As all of us are vitiated by sin, we can only be odious to God, and that not from tyrannical cruelty but by the fairest reckoning of justice. But if all whom the Lord predestines to death are by condition of nature subject to the judgment of death, of what injustice toward themselves may they complain? (III.xxiii.3 [950])

These two qualifications must be emphasized, for they will always be muted, or even ignored, by a reading of Calvin's thought which turns on the austerity of a remote deity, capriciously selecting now this one, now that one, and rejecting all others. Such a reading is not true to a theological creativity that would finally rest the case for election at the culmination of the discussion of life in relationship to God the Holy Spirit. It is precisely the relationship to God in the present tense that denies the very speculation so intrinsic to the attempt to understand the priority of grace in the redemption of humanity.

The title of chapter xxiv focuses precisely the genuine ambiguity of Calvin's struggle to delineate the depths of the doctrine of election: "Election Is Confirmed by God's Call; Moreover, the Wicked Bring Upon Themselves the Just Destruction to Which They Are Destined." If one moves *from* the power of God *to* the promise of that ultimate love which is the heart of the gospel, a perfect balance between the elect and the damned must be maintained. This is enshrined in the doctrine of double predestination. The chapter title suggests that this perfect balance will be the subject matter now to be explored, and the opening lines of the chapter point inexorably in that direction:

> bBut to make the matter clearer, we must deal with both the calling of the elect and the blinding and hardening of the wicked. (III.xxiv.1 [964])

Such, though, is not the manner in which this remarkable chapter takes shape. By now it should be expected that Calvin's emphasis is upon the positive point, despite all that he says about the rejected. The fact is that the only certainty he wishes to assert— indeed, the only conviction he can vigorously maintain—concerns the calling of the elect. Here alone is the only certainty the elect may claim:

> bAs it is wrong to make the force of election contingent upon faith in the gospel, by which we feel that it appertains to us, so we shall be following the best order if, in seeking the certainty of our election, we cling to those latter signs which are sure attestations of it. (III.xxiv.4 [968])

To do this we must be clear on where *not* to turn, and this is decisive because our compulsions are really the work of Satan, leading only to the desperation of doubt. Note carefully how this is said, for it will lead to an incisive conclusion:

> bSatan has no more grievous or dangerous temptation to dishearten believers than when he unsettles them with doubt about their election, while at the same time he arouses them with a wicked desire to seek it outside the way. (III.xxiv.4 [968])

We are lured in a false direction, one that intensifies doubt itself. We seek to penetrate the

depths of ultimacy, and when we fail in this, as
inexorably we must, an ultimate doubt—one worthy
of being ascribed to Satan—sets in:

> ᵇI call it "seeking outside the way" when mere man
> attempts to break into the inner recesses of divine
> wisdom, and tries to penetrate even to highest
> eternity, in order to find out what decision has
> been made concerning himself at God's judgment
> seat. (III.xxiv.4 [968])

This is a false lead that only the redeemed may
attempt. How could anyone else care? The compulsive anxiety in the old question "Am I truly saved?"
can arise only by doubting its basis. This is the irony
of that anxiety which weak faith can generate. And it
is all the more devastating since it is pervasively
irrepressible. "Rare indeed is the mind that is not
repeatedly struck with this thought: whence comes
your salvation but from God's election?" Accordingly,
the basic question asserts itself: "Now, what revela-
tion do you have of your election?" (III.xxiv.4 [969]).
The very experience to which we have seen Calvin
appeal is itself the locus of the devastating work of
Satan.

> ᵇTruly, I should desire no surer argument to
> confirm how basely persons of this sort imagine
> predestination than that very experience, because
> the mind could not be infected with a more
> pestilential error than that which overwhelms and
> unsettles the conscience from its peace and tran-
> quillity toward God. (III.xxiv.4 [969])

Even Calvin cannot have it both ways. If the
experience of belief is the only arena within which the

certainty of election is to be found, it is also the arena within which doubt is so forceful. What can be said, then? How can our attention be redemptively focused, away from doubt, and on toward fulfillment? The answer that is suggested is Calvin at his best:

> ᵇConsequently, if we fear shipwreck, we must carefully avoid this rock, against which no one is ever dashed without destruction. Even though discussion about predestination is likened to a dangerous sea, still, in traversing it, one finds safe and calm—I also add pleasant—sailing unless he willfully desire to endanger himself. For just as those engulf themselves in a deadly abyss who, to make their election more certain, investigate God's eternal plan apart from his Word, so those who rightly and duly examine it as it is contained in his Word reap the inestimable fruit of comfort. Let this, therefore, be the way of our inquiry: to begin with God's call, and to end with it. (III.xxiv.4 [969])

Thus speculation is not the clue, relationship is. This triumph of the relational dimension of the gospel is surely rooted in Calvin's knowledge of the Bible and thus his own assimilation of Hebraic insights. God is known only in God's relation to us. If this is central, the calling of God will truly be both the beginning and the end of all that we have to say. Gone now is any argument from a symmetrical balance between elect and rejected. Present now, overwhelmingly so, is the appeal to the gospel itself.

> ᵇFirst, if we seek God's fatherly mercy and kindly heart, we should turn our eyes to Christ, on whom alone God's Spirit rests. . . . Now what is the purpose of election but that we, adopted as sons by

our Heavenly Father, may obtain salvation and
immortality by his favor? No matter how much you
toss it about and mull it over, you will discover that
its final bounds extend no farther. . . . But if we
have been chosen in him, we shall not find
assurance of our election in ourselves; and not
even in God the Father, if we conceive him as
severed from his Son. Christ, then, is the mirror
wherein we must, and without self-deception may,
contemplate our own election. (III.xxiv.5 [970])

The conclusion to which we pointed a moment
ago is now at hand. The decisive speculation that
Calvin reverses has to do with *thinking of God the Father
conceived as separated from the Son.* Only those who
have heard, and doubted, the gospel can achieve this
error. Even in a Christian doctrine of God there is
nothing but dreadful doubt in contemplating God the
Father apart from God the Son. In a time shaped and
inspired by theological reflection in feminist perspec-
tives this must be stated forcefully. The ultimate one
cannot be known apart from the relationships the
gospel proclaims and promises. Christ is indeed the
mirror in which we see ourselves.

This is what it means to begin and end all we have
to say with our calling:

bIf we desire to know whether God cares for our
salvation, let us inquire whether he has entrusted
us to Christ, whom he has established as the sole
Savior of all his people. If we still doubt whether
we have been received by Christ into his care and
protection, he meets that doubt when he willingly
offers himself as shepherd, and declares that we
shall be numbered among his flock if we hear his
voice [John 10:3]. Let us therefore embrace Christ,
who is graciously offered to us, and comes to meet

us. He will reckon us in his flock and enclose us within his fold. (III.xxiv.6 [971–972])

In this certainty alone, we must abide; with this conviction alone, we are to live; to the experience of faith alone, we are to appeal and, in this appeal, live:

> bFinally, we are taught by this very experience that call and faith are of little account unless persever-ance be added; and this does not happen to all. (III.xxiv.6 [972])

Thus chapter xxiv of the *Institutes* finds its primary concern to be the explication of the experience of the elect, the experience, that is, of life in the midst of the hearing of the gospel. It is in these terms that those who do not hear are to be pondered. Calvin's choice delineation is one that rings true to the experience of not only the hearing of the gospel but of the attempt to proclaim that same gospel. Here too, false pride gives way before the prevailing insight—salvation is ours by grace alone:

> bThe supreme Judge, then, makes way for his predestination when he leaves in blindness those whom he has once condemned and deprived of participation in his light. Of the former effect there are daily proofs as well as many proofs in Scripture. If the same sermon is preached, say, to a hundred people, twenty receive it with the ready obedience of faith, while the rest hold it valueless, or laugh, or hiss, or loathe it. If anyone should reply that this diversity arises out of their malice and perverseness, I still will not be satisfied, because the nature of the former would be occu-pied with the same malice if God did not correct it by his goodness. eTherefore, we shall always be

> confused unless Paul's question comes to mind:
> Who distinguishes you? [I Cor. 4:7]. By this he
> means that some excel others not by their own
> virtue but by God's grace alone. (III.xxiv.12 [979])

To say that the doctrine of election makes sense
only in the context of experiencing it puts the
emphasis where it belongs—on the responsibility
which the hearing of the gospel carries with it. Truly
to hear the gospel is to know the necessity of
proclaiming it. But how does one maintain the
perseverance this requires in the face of what we have
just heard Calvin say? Only by way of a confidence
that rests in the power of the God who loves. It is
instructive that this is the point at which Calvin takes
up "The Final Resurrection," the concluding chapter
of Book III—instructive because this chapter *was not
needed* in the great christological chapter vi of Book
II. For Calvin, the resurrection of Jesus Christ is more
significant than simply being a proof of the claim that
the Mediator is true God and true humanity. Rather,
it is the inexhaustible symbol of the fact that our
confidence in the power of God entails the hope
intrinsic to the gospel of the love of God. At the
pinnacle of the claims of the gospel we are confronted
with the ultimate revision of our faith. Calvin himself
says that faith in the resurrection of Christ is prior to
our convictions concerning the power of God:

> [e(b)]It is difficult to believe that bodies, when
> consumed with rottenness, will at length be raised
> up in their season. Therefore, although many of
> the philosophers declared souls immortal, few
> approved the resurrection of the flesh. Even
> though there was no excuse for this point of view,

we are nevertheless reminded by it that it is something too hard for men's minds to apprehend. Scripture provides two helps by which faith may overcome this great obstacle: one in the parallel of Christ's resurrection; the other in the omnipotence of God. (III.xxv.3 [990])

Here Calvin himself moves *from* the claim of the gospel *to* the understanding of the power of God. More than that, precisely what is this "parallel" to Christ's resurrection? It is our own:

e(b)Now whenever we consider the resurrection, let Christ's image come before us. In the nature which he took from us he so completed the course of mortal life that now, having obtained immortality, he is the pledge of our coming resurrection. (III.xxv.3 [990])

Now there recurs the use of the same astonishing metaphor of the *mirror*, which, as we have seen, informs one of the decisive turning points of the mighty chapter on election.

eChrist rose again that he might have us as companions in the life to come. He was raised by the Father, inasmuch as he was Head of the church, from which the Father in no way allows him to be severed. He was raised by the power of the Holy Spirit, the Quickener of us in common with him. . . . As we have said that in this mirror the living image of the resurrection is visible to us, so is it a firm foundation to support our minds, provided we are not wearied or irked with a longer delay; for our task is not to measure minutes of time as we please but patiently to wait until God in his own good time restores his Kingdom. (III.xxv.3 [991])

And so the conviction of the elect emerges. The God of love is powerful. This is good news indeed. And *this* power we proclaim, for, as Calvin insists,

> [e]let us remember that no one is truly persuaded of the coming resurrection unless he is seized with wonder, and ascribes to the power of God its due glory. (III.xxv.4 [993])

How is this gospel to be present in the human realm? For Calvin's answer to this question we must turn to Book IV and hear him speak of the church and civil government.

CHAPTER FOUR

Reflections on the Church and Civil Government
—Book IV

XIII. The church is the providential instrument of God and is to be understood as God's accommodation to us.

As we have had cause to remark at many instances, so here: Calvin's thought unfolds in a massive spiral and in such a way that at virtually every juncture all that goes before depends upon what is about to be said. This varies in its intensity, but the point could hardly be more significant than it is in the relationship between the discussion in Book IV and the preceding discussions in Books I, II, and III. Calvin's thought presupposes a strong doctrine of the church, and this understanding generates an equally robust understanding of civil government. Review, for example, our discussions of the threefold office of Christ, noting how we are involved in the operation of each of these offices. If a doctrine of the church is not forthcoming, the cogency of Calvin's contribution to the understanding of Christology is undermined.

Given this, for it is there for all who read carefully, it is truly striking that in the initial note that accompanies Book IV we are alerted to the fact that "until our century this part of his theology has attracted little attention from his interpreters" (1011 n.1). Clearly, the issues at hand were of the utmost significance for Calvin himself. This he sought to indicate in the title for Book IV, "The External Means or Aids by Which God Invites Us Into the Society of Christ and Holds Us Therein." We are lost without these external means; they are hardly of secondary significance then. And this accounts for the forceful lines with which Book IV commences:

> [e]As explained in the previous book, it is by the faith in the gospel that Christ becomes ours and we are made partakers of the salvation and eternal blessedness brought by him. Since, however, in our ignorance and sloth (to which I add fickleness of disposition) we need outward helps to beget and increase faith within us, and advance it to its goal, God has also added these aids that he may provide for our weakness. [e(b)]And in order that the preaching of the gospel might flourish, he deposited this treasure in the church. (IV.i.1 [1011–1012])

Take careful note that the need for the church is rooted in our weakness. The knowledge of human limitation, not the fact of human sin, is the ground of the necessity for the church. In a fashion exactly analogous to Calvin's central christological affirmations, where human limitation is the ground of the need for the Mediator, so here: The church is God's providential accommodation to our capacity:

> eShut up as we are in the prison house of our flesh, we have not yet attained angelic rank. God, therefore, in his wonderful providence accommodating himself to our capacity, has prescribed a way for us, though still far off, to draw near to him. (IV.i.1 [1012])

Life in the church has to do with participation in election. The way things stand in the 1559 edition of the *Institutes* this is the only way to put the matter, given the experiential character of the doctrine of election itself, as it finally emerges in Calvin's reflection. Thus, life in the church has to do with the benefits of God, which, let us recall yet again, is intrinsic to that true piety (I.ii.1 [41]) which Calvin seeks to elaborate in the argument of the *Institutes* as a whole:

> e(b)Now, it is very important for us to know what benefit we shall gain from this. The basis on which we believe the church is that we are fully convinced we are members of it. b(a)In this way our salvation rests upon sure and firm supports. (IV.i.3 [1015])

Two factors yield this conviction, and each of them turns on the experience of the faithful:

> aFirst, it stands by God's election, and cannot waver or fail any more than his eternal providence can. b(a)Secondly, it has in a way been joined to the steadfastness of Christ, who will no more allow his believers to be estranged from him than that his members be rent and torn asunder. (IV.i.3 [1015])

In elaborating the confidence he asserts, Calvin adds a decisive observation. Our confidence depends on God alone; it is not the function of a doctrine concerning those who do not believe:

> bHere we are not bidden to distinguish between reprobate and elect—that is for God alone, not for us, to do—but to establish with certainty in our hearts that all those who, by the kindness of God the Father, through the working of the Holy Spirit, have entered into fellowship with Christ, are set apart as God's property and personal possession; and that when we are of their number we share that great grace. (IV.i.3 [1015–1016])

Our certainty, however, unfolds only in the midst of the ambiguities of life in this realm, where the very distinction between elect and reprobate, known only to God, is beyond any final determination on our part. This is what forces Calvin's attempt to distinguish between the *visible* and the *invisible* church. On the one hand, the church consists of "all the elect from the beginning of the world" (IV.i.7 [1021]). On the other hand, "the name 'church' designates the whole multitude of men spread over the earth who profess to worship one God and Christ" (IV.i.7 [1021]). It is the latter realm, the only one we know, that is marked by ambiguity:

> cIn this church are mingled many hypocrites who have nothing of Christ but the name and outward appearance. There are very many ambitious, greedy, envious persons, evil speakers, and some of quite unclean life. Such are tolerated for a time either because they cannot be convicted by a competent tribunal or because a vigorous disci-

> pline does not always flourish as it ought. (IV.i.7 [1021–1022])

Ambiguous though it is, the latter church, the only church visible to us, is that very external aid so necessary to our salvation, which, along with civil government, is the subject for discussion in Book IV.

How is the visible church to be discerned? This is the juncture at which Calvin introduces his formulation of the marks of the church:

> [a]Wherever we see the Word of God purely preached and heard, and the sacraments administered according to Christ's institution, there, it is not to be doubted, a church of God exists. (IV.i.9 [1023])

These lines are present from the 1536 edition of the *Institutes* forward. Moreover, they are paralleled in the letter of dedication to King Francis which introduced that initial edition:

> Our controversy turns on these hinges: first, they contend that the form of the church is always apparent and observable. Secondly, they set this form in the see of the Roman Church and its hierarchy. We, on the contrary, affirm that the chuch can exist without any visible appearance, and that its appearance is not contained within that outward magnificence which they foolishly admire. Rather, it has quite another mark: namely, the pure preaching of God's Word and the lawful administration of the sacraments. (Pages 24–25).

We do indeed need before us this passage from the letter if we would understand the careful precision that attends Calvin's doctrine of the church. The only church *we* know in this realm is the visible church.

The struggle with Rome had to do with the nature of this visibility. It still does. Rome, then and now, locates the authenticating visibility of the church in the hierarchy. Calvin, in complete accord with the Lutherans (see 1023 n. 18), locates it in the preaching and the hearing of the word and the biblically ordered administering of the sacraments. It is *this* visible church that is the concern of the remainder of the first nineteen chapters of Book IV.

Given the marks of the church as Calvin understands them, it is no surprise that the central emphasis in his discussion of the visible church that we know has to do with the office of the ministry. The basic point in this emphasis is the insistence upon the *instrumental* character of this office. God uses human effort as a workman uses his tools. Calvin's full statement here is crucial:

> cNow we must speak of the order by which the Lord willed his church to be governed. He alone should rule and reign in the church as well as have authority or pre-eminence in it, and this authority should be exercised and administered by his Word alone. Nevertheless, because he does not dwell among us in visible presence [Matt. 26:11], we have said that he uses the ministry of men to declare openly his will to us by mouth, as a sort of delegated work, not by transferring to them his right and honor, but only that through their mouths he may do his own work—just as a workman uses a tool to do his work. (IV.iii.1 [1053])

Calvin immediately lists three reasons why God "prefers" to do through human ministry what could be done without human agency. First, this "declares his regard for us." Second, intrinsic to this arrangement is "the best and most useful exercise in humility." And third, "nothing fosters mutual love more fittingly than for men to be bound together with this bond" (IV.iii.1 [1053–1054]).

The elaboration of the second of these reasons is truly memorable:

> ᶜThis is the best and most useful exercise in humility, when he accustoms us to obey his Word, even though it be preached through men like us and sometimes even by those of lower worth than we. If he spoke from heaven, it would not be surprising if his sacred oracles were to be reverently received without delay by the ears and minds of all. For who would not dread the presence of his power? Who would not be stricken down at the sight of such great majesty? Who would not be confounded at such boundless splendor? But when a puny man risen from the dust speaks in God's name, at this point we best evidence our piety and obedience toward God if we show ourselves teachable toward his minister, although he excels us in nothing. It was for this reason, then, that he hid the treasure of his heavenly wisdom in weak and earthen vessels [II Cor. 4:7] in order to prove more surely how much we should esteem it. (IV.iii.1 [1054])

In fact, "memorable" is too tame a word to measure the significance of this passage. It can be read sentimentally, or even with a sense of irony over the mighty Calvin being instructed by some "puny man risen from the dust." The insight includes this stroke, but its depths will be reached only when we read the passage with Calvin's version of the marks of the church in mind. Recall that these turn on the right preaching *and hearing* of the word. Hearing the word is a matter of the faithful imagination. Even the mightiest learning has no monopoly on the capacity to trigger this response. When one truly hears God's word, there can be no denying its power. And this hearing involves, but is not limited to, the most rigorous attempt to understand the word in its infinite reach.

So it is that the third insight achieves its cogency. Why is it that "nothing fosters mutual love more fittingly than for men to be bound together with this bond"—why, that is, is the fact that God works through the instrumentality of human agency so important?

> ᶜThe Lord has therefore bound his church together with a knot that he foresaw would be the strongest means of keeping unity, while he entrusted to men the teaching of salvation and everlasting life in order that through their hands it might be communicated to the rest. (IV.iii.1 [1054])

We are dependent upon each other for the words that promise eternal life. We can hardly be more closely bound up, one with another.

Only now is Calvin willing to risk stating his extremely high view of the office of the ministry. Having quoted Ephesians, he observes:

> ᶜPaul shows by these words that this human ministry which God uses to govern the church is the chief sinew by which believers are held together in one body. . . . For neither the light and

> heat of the sun, nor food and drink, are so
> necessary to nourish and sustain the present life as
> the apostolic and pastoral office is necessary to
> preserve the church on earth. (IV.iii.2 [1055])

Thus the church is understood as a function of God's providence. It is nothing less than the accommodation of ultimacy to human limits, and this understanding turns on the high office of the ministry. This is the true apostolicity. This is what it means to focus everything on the pastoral function of leadership in the church. The body is linked in all its parts by this "chief sinew."

Calvin understood the offices of leadership in the church to be five in number: apostles, prophets, evangelists, pastors, and teachers. The first three were not permanent in his way of thinking, for they had to do with the initial establishment of the church. In this connection, note that by "evangelists" he meant, following Luke 10:1, persons such as Luke, Timothy, and Titus "whom Christ appointed in the second place after the apostles" (IV.iii.4 [1057]). Note further that from time to time apostles and evangelists would be summoned to call the church back "from the rebellion of Antichrist" (IV.iii.4 [1057]). Here he would not hesitate to designate Luther as such a person (see 1057 n. 4). But having said this, Calvin was clear that the ongoing life of the church depends upon the functioning of the offices of pastors and teachers. And in his formulation the former of these was the more inclusive of the two:

> cNext come pastors and teachers, whom the
> church can never go without. There is, I believe,

> this difference between them: teachers are not put
> in charge of discipline, or administering the
> sacraments, or warnings and exhortations, but
> only of Scriptural interpretation—to keep doctrine
> whole and pure among believers. But the pastoral
> office includes all these functions within itself.
> (IV.iii.4 [1057])

Note carefully that at the head of the list for which
pastors, but not teachers, are responsible is the matter
of *discipline*. We have often noted the profoundly
Hebraic character of Calvin's thought, its relational
and ethical dimensions playing decisive roles at
almost every turn. Thus, given the ambiguity of the
visible church, it is inexorable that discipline will play
a crucial role in his discussion of the only church we
know. In turning to this matter, however, we must
not make the mistake of overstating its clearly massive
significance for Calvin's argument, for, important
though it is, he himself did not regard discipline as
one of the marks of the church. (The subsequent
tradition did; see 1023 n. 18).

Calvin discusses church discipline as a function of
"the power of the keys" considered as a matter of
"spiritual discipline" (IV.xii.1 [1229]). It will suffice
for us to reckon with the "common discipline,"
applicable to both "clergy and people," though we
must note that, in addition to this, added strictures
concerning the former are taken up in some detail
later (see IV.xii.22ff. [1248ff.]). Once again, experience informs his initial point:

> ᶜIf no society, indeed, no house which has even a
> small family, can be kept in proper condition
> without discipline, it is much more necessary in

the church, whose condition should be as ordered as possible. (IV.xii.1 [1229–1230])

In a manner reminiscent of the progress toward the third use of the law, Calvin epitomizes the function he envisions as follows:

ᶜDiscipline is like a bridle to restrain and tame those who rage against the doctrine of Christ; or like a spur to arouse those of little inclination; and also sometimes like a father's rod to chastise mildly and with the gentleness of Christ's Spirit those who have more seriously lapsed. (IV.xii.1 [1230])

All this unfolds in three steps: the first, that of "private admonition"; the second, admonition "in the presence of witnesses," plus a summons before "the tribunal of the church, that is, the assembly of the elders." The hope of this second stage is that "public authority" may generate that reverence for the church which will lead to submission and obedience. If these two moves fail, expulsion from the church is the only option:

ᶜIf he is not even subdued by this but perseveres in his wickedness, then Christ commands that, as a despiser of the church, he be removed from the believers' fellowship [Matt. 18:15, 17]. (IV.xii.2 [1231])

These opening steps in Calvin's discussion of church discipline are the direct implications of his citation of "the power of the keys," for the decisive question has to do with the understanding of the extreme case, that of excommunication. This must be focused carefully. "In such corrections and excommunication, the church has three ends in view" (IV.xii.5

[1232]). The first has a double purpose, pivoting on the honor due to God and the necessity of safeguarding the sacrament from profanation by being offered thoughtlessly:

> [a]The first is that they who lead a filthy and infamous life may not be called Christians, to the dishonor of God, as if his holy church [cf. Eph. 5:25–26] were a conspiracy of wicked and abandoned men. . . . [c]And here also we must preserve the order of the Lord's Supper, that it may not be profaned by being administered indiscriminately. (IV.xii.5 [1232])

The second purpose is "that the good be not corrupted," and the third "that those overcome by shame for their baseness begin to repent" (IV.xii.5 [1233]).

Compact though these formulations are, they should be given close attention, and would that all who continue to insist on the inherited view of Calvin's ruthless austerity could be commanded to listen closely. The function of excommunication is *positive* for him. The third purpose of this extreme judgment must inform the first two, lest their real source, "the gentleness of Christ's Spirit," as we have heard him put it (IV.xii.1 [1230]), be forgotten. Calvin went to great lengths to emphasize precisely this fact.

> [b]Although excommunication also punishes the man, it does so in such a way that, by forewarning him of his future condemnation, it may call him back to salvation. But if that be obtained, reconciliation and restoration to communion await him. [c]Moreover, anathema is very rarely or never used. [a]Accordingly, though ecclesiastical discipline does not permit us to live familiarly or have intimate

contact with excommunicated persons, we ought nevertheless to strive by whatever means we can in order that they may turn to a more virtuous life and may return to the society and unity of the church. bSo the apostle also teaches: "Do not look upon them as enemies, but warn them as brothers" [II Thess. 3:15]. Unless this gentleness is maintained in both private and public censures, there is danger lest we soon slide down from discipline to butchery. (IV.xii.10 [1238])

Once again, just as was the case, for example, in the discussion of the third use of the law (differentiating Calvin from Luther in such a significant way), here we are in touch with an aspect of Calvin's thought that would prove to be of great significance for subsequent developments. This is the element of his understanding of church discipline that veers in the direction of the Anabaptist vision of the holy community. In Calvin's view excommunication is not to be turned over to civil authority. It is a matter of the church's own self-disciplining capacities.

As we have seen, for Calvin the marks of the church have to do with the preaching and the hearing of the word of God and the administering of the sacraments according to Christ's institution. Only now, with all that has gone before well in place, does Calvin turn to the understanding of the sacraments. These are two in number, Baptism, and the Lord's Supper. The crucial issues for us are to be found in the initial chapter that introduces the discussion of the sacraments, viz., chapter xiv. It should be noted, however, that a full chapter is devoted to each of the two sacraments, plus a polemical chapter on the papal mass, and a detailed discussion rejecting each of the other five sacraments that are central to the system in operation in the Roman church.

Calvin's initial move is to make common cause with Augustine in treating the sacrament as an outward sign of an inward grace:

> [a]First, we must consider what a sacrament is. [c(a)]It seems to me that a simple and proper definition would be to say that it is an outward sign by which the Lord seals on our consciences the promises of his good will toward us in order to sustain the weakness of our faith; and we in turn attest our piety toward him in the presence of the Lord and of his angels before men. Here is another briefer definition: one may call it a testimony of divine grace toward us, confirmed by an outward sign, [c]with mutual attestation of our piety toward him. Whichever of these definitions you may choose, it does not differ in meaning from that of Augustine, who teaches that a sacrament is "a visible sign of a sacred thing," or "a visible form of an invisible grace." (IV.xiv.1 [1277])

Why this addition, for addition it is, to the word of the gospel? Here, at the very outset of all that Calvin has to say regarding the second mark of the church, we encounter the decisive component of his thought. The sacraments are extensions of the word. That is to say, in the central combination at the very heart of the liturgical nature of Christian faith, word has precedence over sacrament, since word explains sacrament and sacrament substantiates and confirms word.

> [a]Now, from the definition that I have set forth we understand that a sacrament is never without a preceding promise but is joined to it as a sort of appendix, with the purpose of confirming and

> sealing the promise itself, and of making it more
> evident to us and in a sense ratifying it. (IV.xiv.3
> [1278])

The sacraments epitomize God's adaptation of grace to our human capacity. Calvin's hyperbole, always present when he contrasts the grace of God and our human limitations, gets in the way of this insight. Despite his adducing of our human weakness necessitating the aids of the sacraments, the deeper base of the sacramental dimensions of the marks of the church has to do with the loving character of God's approach to us. Our experience is bodily in character. It is this that accounts for the fact that the sacraments *necessarily accompany the word*. Even in adducing our weaknesses as necessitating the sacraments the positive note comes in:

> [a]By this means God provides first for our ignorance
> and dullness, then for our weakness. Yet, properly
> speaking, it is not so much needed to confirm his
> Sacred Word as to establish us in faith in it.
> (IV.xiv.3 [1278])

And it is the positive note that overwhelms the hyperbole of negativism, with the introduction, yet once more, of the remarkable metaphor of the mirror:

> [a]Here our merciful Lord, according to his infinite
> kindness, so tempers himself to our capacity that,
> since we are creatures who always creep on the
> ground, cleave to the flesh, and, do not think about
> or even conceive of anything spiritual, he conde-
> scends to lead us to himself even by these earthly
> elements, and to set before us in the flesh a mirror
> of spiritual blessings. [c]For if we were incorporeal
> (as Chrysostom says), he would give us these very

things naked and incorporeal. Now, because we
have souls engrafted in bodies, he imparts spiritual
things under visible ones. ªNot that the gifts set
before us in the sacraments are bestowed with the
natures of the things, but that they have been
marked with this signification by God. (IV.xiv.3
[1278])

How do we know that this is so? How can we truly
affirm that water, bread, wine are indeed outward
signs of an inward grace? On what basis can we claim
that grace has been so adapted to the concrete earthly
and bodily realm within which the only life we know
is lived out? Only by the proclamation of the word
that, thus strengthened, speaks with unmistakable
conviction:

ᶜWe ought to understand the word not as one
whispered without meaning and without faith, a
mere noise, like a magic incantation, which has the
force to consecrate the element. Rather, it should,
when preached, make us understand what the
visible sign means. (IV.xiv.4 [1279])

This explains the colossal liturgical risk run by the
Reformers, especially those of the Reformed tradition. The altar is pushed out from the wall and
becomes a table, sharing in a secondary place with the
primacy of the pulpit the center of worship:

ᶜYou see how the sacrament requires preaching to
beget faith. And we need not labor to prove this
when it is perfectly clear what Christ did, what he
commanded us to do, what the apostles followed,
and what the purer church observed. ᵉIndeed, it
was known even from the beginning of the world
that whenever God gave a sign to the holy

patriarchs it was inseparably linked to doctrine, without which our senses would have been stunned in looking at the bare sign. ᶜAccordingly, when we hear the sacramental word mentioned, let us understand the promise, proclaimed in a clear voice by the minister, to lead the people by the hand wherever the sign tends and directs us. (IV.xiv.4 [1279–1280])

Word and sacrament—these are the marks of the church. Where Christ is there they are; and this is why where they are Christ is. In that order alone, given the Reformation, dare we risk the radical change in the heart of the liturgy that the Reformers in general, and this one in particular, so unequivocally demanded. Does one go from word to sacrament, or from sacrament to word? In the irrevocably ecumenical era that is happily ours we can now lift this issue into the prominence it deserves. The experiential depths of the manner in which one receives the faith leaves indelible marks on her or him. We are shaped one way or the other, to such an extent that for most of us our liturgical homes cannot be shifted. And for those of us who do make the transition from the one to the other far more profound wrenching is involved than is usually admitted. Moreover, for all the yearning that might be felt for whichever is the other option, the supposed new strengths that change is to bring are bought with great price. Those believers whose birthright is in one of the great eucharistic communions will go from sacrament to word. Calvin reversed this with an unshakable conviction. *From* word *to* sacrament we must go, if the gospel is indeed ours. The risk of proclamation both needs, and can depend upon, the visible signs of inward grace. But risk it remains, on this side of the great beyond. As we shall see, precisely this same risky conviction informs his discussion of civil government.

XIV. By analogy, civil government is also to be understood as the instrument of God for the good of humanity.

Every edition of the *Institutes* culminates with a section on civil government. This reflects the fact that Calvin's early training was in law, and the progression is always that of moving from a discussion of the church to the treatment of the political realm. In the 1536 edition the material now before us was "linked with the [chapter] on 'Christian Freedom' (III.xix), which, in substance, formed the first part of ch. vi [of that edition] . . . and was followed in the same long chapter by a section on ecclesiastical power and one bearing the title of the present chapter and essentially of the same content" (1485 n. 2). As we have seen, the culmination of Book III is now the progression from prayer, to the extended treatment of election, in its new place in the argument of the *Institutes* as a whole, to a chapter on "The Final Resurrection." The fact is that this new progression strengthens the connection between Calvin's understanding of Christian freedom and his treatment of "Civil Government," as the final chapter of Book IV is entitled. The doctrine of election is now understood as the culmination of the insights concerning life in the context of the Spirit. Thus, its true significance, as we have seen, concerns the *responsibility* of the elect in the proclamation of the gospel. With an abiding conviction rooted in the experience of faith in the final resurrection, this sense of responsibility carries even farther the positive relationship to the contexts of the life of men and women already present in the treatments of the third use of the law and the relationship between sanctification and justification. This, in turn, sets the stage for the discussion of the church and civil government in Book IV.

Of the twenty chapters that constitute Book IV the first nineteen are concerned with the church, the twentieth with the political realm. The primary reason for this seemingly disproportionate treatment has to do with the fact that the understanding of the political realm being developed is exactly analogous to the understanding of the church. In that sense the way has been prepared for the discussion now at hand.

At the outset Calvin clearly intimates the positive character of his view:

> [e]Although this topic seems by nature alien to the spiritual doctrine of faith which I have undertaken to discuss, what follows will show that I am right in joining them, in fact, that necessity compels me to do so. This is especially true since, from one side, insane and barbarous men furiously strive to overturn this divinely established order; while, on the other side, the flatterers of princes, immoderately praising their power, do not hesitate to set them against the rule of God himself. Unless both these evils are checked, purity of faith will perish. Besides, it is of no slight importance to us to know how lovingly God has provided in this respect for mankind, that greater zeal for piety may flourish in us to attest our gratefulness. (IV.xx.1 [1485–1486])

Neither the extremism of an Anabaptist denial of the significance of the political order nor an absolutizing of political power may be countenanced. But note well, neither may we overlook that what is at hand has to do with the manner in which "God has provided in this respect for mankind" and that this, in turn, relates to the possibility of "greater zeal for piety."

Calvin insists "that Christ's spiritual Kingdom and the civil jurisdiction are things completely distinct" (IV.xx.1 [1486]). But he also insists that "this distinction does not lead us to consider the whole nature of government a thing polluted, which has nothing to do with Christian men" (IV.xx.2 [1487]). Why not?

> [a]Spiritual government, indeed, is already initiating in us upon earth certain beginnings of the Heavenly Kingdom, and in this mortal and fleeting life affords a certain forecast of an immortal and incorruptible blessedness. Yet civil government has as its appointed end, so long as we live among men, [e]to cherish and protect the outward worship of God, to defend sound doctrine of piety and the position of the church, [a]to adjust our life to the society of men, to form our social behavior to civil righteousness, to reconcile us with one another, and to promote general peace and tranquillity. (IV.xx.2 [1487])

This specification of responsibility is fascinating. The protection of the church and the defense of sound doctrine and piety overlap with adjustment of life to the human society and the promotion of the general peace and tranquillity. The intersection is *necessary*, and its necessity will disappear only with the arrival of the eschaton; for in this present life human nature is intrinsically political in character. So, Calvin goes on immediately to assert that

> [a]all of this I admit to be superfluous, if God's Kingdom, such as it is now among us, wipes out the present life. But if it is God's will that we go as pilgrims upon the earth while we aspire to the true fatherland, and if the pilgrimage requires such helps, those who take these from man deprive him of his very humanity. (IV.xx.2 [1487])

Just as had been the case in the discussion of the church, so now. We must have a clear understanding of the crucial office within the structure at hand. The office of the magistrate relates to civil government in the same way that the office of the ministry relates to the church. First of all, we must know that

> [a]the Lord has not only testified that the office of the magistrate is approved by and acceptable to him, but he also sets out its dignity with the most honorable titles and marvelously commends it to us. (IV.xx.4 [1489])

Immediately following this passage Calvin quotes at length from the Old Testament (with a single passage from the New), in order then to comment as follows:

> [a]This amounts to the same thing as to say: it has not come about by human perversity that the authority over all things on earth is in the hands of kings and other rulers, but by divine providence and holy ordinance. For God was pleased so to rule the affairs of men, [b]inasmuch as he is present with them and also presides over the making of laws and the exercising of equity in courts of justice. (IV.xx.4 [1489])

The office of the magistrate is thus grounded in the providence of God.

Again we are in the presence of a distinctive emphasis in the thought of Calvin, one that leaves a permanent mark on the subsequent development of the Reformed tradition. We have already come to terms with the way in which Calvin moved with, and then beyond, Luther on the third use of the law and on the relationship between sanctification and justification. But what is before us now is the most decisive of the differentiations between these two key figures in the emergence of Reformation thought. Calvin rooted civil government in the providence of God, not, as did Luther, in the sinfulness of humanity. Only so can he see civil government as the parallel of the church as an external aid by which God's grace operates in the midst of life in this world. And only so can he speak of political office in such positive terms:

> [a]No one ought to doubt that civil authority is a calling, not only holy and lawful before God, but also the most sacred and by far the most honorable of all callings in the whole life of mortal men. (IV.xx.4 [1490])

Thus the high view of the calling of political office is on a par with the office of the ministry which, as we have seen, Calvin called "the chief sinew by which believers are held together in one body" (IV.iii.2 [1055]). With this accolade goes heavy responsibility and an equally glowing figure of speech. In fulfilling their responsibilities the magistrates are under the severe discipline of remembering that they are "vicars of God."

^aTo sum up, if they remember that they are vicars of God, they should watch with all care, earnestness, and diligence, to represent in themselves to men some image of divine providence, protection, goodness, benevolence, and justice. (IV.xx.6 [1491])

So Calvin answers his own rhetorical question: "How will they have the boldness to pronounce an unjust sentence, by that mouth which they know has been appointed an instrument of divine truth?" (IV.xx.6 [1491]). And so he parallels the instrumentality of the pastoral office with the instrumentality of the magistracy. Thus church and civil government, pivoting on the parallel understandings of the offices upon which they depend, are the twin channels of God's providential ordering of the lives of women and men.

How far can this sense of the providential character of the office of the magistrate be taken? As far as the necessity of reflecting on the question of political resistance to the oppression of tyrannical rulers—to this length Calvin goes, and by now the contrast with Luther, and the subsequent deep-seated differentiation between the Reformed and Lutheran traditions, reaches one of its most significant developments. The elaboration will seem tame indeed to modern minds, unless we take into account the fact that the development of a city republic in Geneva, with the consequent differentiation of this kind of body politic as over against the empire, to say nothing of the Roman church, was well under way long before Calvin took up his work there. Clearly, then, here is one of those instances when context and creativity conspire to yield what would

prove to be a decisive turning in the history of
Christian social thought.

Given his high conception of the significance of
the office of the magistrate, Calvin will countenance
no disorderly rejection of magisterial authority:

> ªLet no man deceive himself here. For since the
> magistrate cannot be resisted without God being
> resisted at the same time, even though it seems
> that an unarmed magistrate can be despised with
> impunity, still God is armed to avenge mightily
> this contempt toward himself. (IV.xx.23 [1511])

If, though, this is really true, then it extends to *all* the
exercises of this same authority. And this principle
can be extended beyond the realms of simply main-
taining the status quo as this pertains to the relationship between the city-based office of the magistrate
and the broader reaches of overarching domains so
much a part of a feudal world about to undergo its
demise. This is the setting for the famous clarification
of the revolutionary power of the so-called inferior
magistracy:

> ªMoreover, under this obedience I include the
> restraint which private citizens ought to bid
> themselves keep in public, that they may not
> deliberately intrude in public affairs, or pointlessly
> invade the magistrate's office, or undertake any-
> thing at all politically. If anything in a public
> ordinance requires amendment, let them not raise
> a tumult, or put their hands to the task—all of them
> ought to keep their hands bound in this respect—
> but let them commit the matter to the judgment of
> the magistrate, whose hand alone here is free. I
> mean, let them not venture on anything without a

> command. For when the ruler gives his command,
> private citizens receive public authority. For as the
> counselors are commonly called the ears and eyes
> of the prince, so may one reasonably speak of those
> whom he has appointed by his command to do
> things, as the hands of the prince. (IV.xx.23 [1511])

How free, then, is the hand of the magistrate? Free enough to lead resistance to higher authority in the name of the people, and in that act powerful enough to ascribe to the people nothing less than the very *public authority* that the office presupposes. This is at best a tiny loophole, but through it would shine enough light for John Knox, Calvin's student, to link the cause of the Reformation to the struggle against Mary Queen of Scots.

The principle at hand is of the utmost significance. Given Calvin's positive understanding of the political realm, an understanding worked out on theological grounds, the logical implication of a theologically ordered understanding of the political revolution inexorably emerges. Here Calvin is far closer to Thomas Aquinas than he is to Luther. To be sure, Calvin's understanding of both church and civil government explicitly runs counter to Thomas's hierarchical view of the relationship between spiritual and temporal power. But Thomas too thought through his points in a manner that ascribed to the political realm a theologically ordered grasp of its positive significance. On the ground of his thought also, therefore, a theologically informed understanding of political revolution inexorably arises. Centuries would come and go before an ecumenical era could truly envision an affinity here that would receive

fresh embodiment in the theologically ordered struggles for liberation that are so much a part of life in the
church and the world today.

The fact is that Calvin's thought can well be ad-
duced in our present efforts. The passage we have just
noted is indeed convoluted, but the theological cogency
involved is clear. And the repetition of precisely this
line of reflection is reduplicated in anything but
ambiguous terms as the final lines of the *Institutes* take
shape. First the forceful limitation is stated:

> ªIf the correction of unbridled despotism is
> the Lord's to avenge, let us not at once think that
> it is entrusted to us, to whom no command has
> been given except to obey and suffer. (IV.xx.31
> [1518])

Immediately, then, the power of the magisterial office
comes before us, with a forceful statement, now, of
the contention that what is at hand is not simply an
option but a faithful necessity if the purpose of this
power is honorable before God:

> ªI am speaking all the while of private individuals.
> For if there are now any magistrates of the people,
> appointed to restrain the willfulness of kings (as in
> ancient times the ephors were set against the
> Spartan kings, or the tribunes of the people against
> the Roman consuls, or the demarchs against the
> senate of the Athenians; and perhaps, as things
> now are, such power as the three estates exercise
> in every realm when they hold their chief assem-
> blies), I am so far from forbidding them to
> withstand, in accordance with their duty, the fierce
> licentiousness of kings, that, if they wink at kings
> who violently fall upon and assault the lowly

common folk, I declare that their dissimulation involves nefarious perfidy, because they dishonestly betray the freedom of the people, of which they know that they have been appointed protectors by God's ordinance. (IV.xx.31 [1519])

Just as the understanding of excommunication is rooted in a positive grasp of the church as a necessary external aid for our hearing and living the gospel, so the incisive delineation of the providential character of magisterial leadership in the resistance against tyranny underscores the fact that civil government too is God's providential gift for the ordering of the lives of women and men. And so, just as that emphasis upon true piety is present at the opening of the massive argument of the *Institutes*, so it is present at the close. The very possibility of resistance to oppression before us is itself one of those benefits of God of which we heard early on (see I.ii.1 [41]). These benefits are ours through the very Immanuel in which God's divinity and our humanity "grow together by mutual connection" (II.xii.1 [464–465]). To grasp the *Institutes* as a whole is to know that these notes sound through the lines and doxology with which this remarkable treatise, in each of its editions, is brought to a close:

aI know with what great and present peril this constancy is menaced, because kings bear defiance with the greatest displeasure, whose "wrath is a messenger of death" [Prov. 16:14], says Solomon. But since this edict has been proclaimed by the heavenly herald, Peter—"We must obey God rather than men" [Acts 5:29]—let us comfort ourselves with the thought that we are rendering that obedience which the Lord requires when we suffer anything rather than turn aside from piety. And that our courage may not grow faint, Paul pricks us with another goad: That we have been redeemed by Christ at so great a price as our redemption cost him, so that we should not enslave ourselves to the wicked desires of men—much less be subject to their impiety [I Cor. 7:23].

GOD BE PRAISED

(IV.xx.32 [1520–1521])

Epilogue

Our study is at an end, but not our labors. A reading of Calvin's *Institutes of the Christian Religion* is one of the most rewarding, and efficient, ways to discover the nature of the theological task. It never ends. Struggling always to plumb the depths of the gospel of Jesus Christ, Calvin's nervous creativity could never really rest. Had he lived on, there is no doubt that a subsequent edition would have emerged. But his further life would be in the great beyond. The subsequent editions will have to be written by us. May our efforts also yield new overtones to the words of the great doxology: *God be praised.*

Index

DATE DUE